Literacy
Through Texts

PEARSON
Longman

Pearson Education Limited

Edinburgh Gate

Harlow

Essex

CM20 2JE

England and Associated Companies throughout the World

ISBN 978 0 582 43441 7

First published 2002

Fifth impression 2008

Printed in China GCC/05

The Publisher's policy is to use paper manufactured from sustainable forests

Designed by Te Marama Design

Project managed by Patricia Moss

Cover illustration by Sam Hadley of Artist Partners Ltd

Illustrations by: Barry Patterson (pages 3–8,10); Tim Clarey (pages 41–43);
David Dean (pages 45–47); Norma Burgin (pages 51–61, 63, 65);
Stephen Player (pages 66–68, 70–74); Hannah Firmin (pages 77–80);
Stephen Player (pages 82–92); Teresa Murfin (pages 105–108); Roger Kent (pages 114–115);
David Semple (pages 138–139, 141); Jon Sayer (page 153–156);
Andy Hammond (pages 168–171, 173–175, 177); David Semple (pages 179–182);
David Roberts (pages 185–187); Sam Hadley (page 200); Peter Allen (pages 201–204);
Bob Warner (pages 205–212); Adam Willis (pages 213–217).

Literacy
Through Texts

Pippa Doran • Lorna Hendry • Steve Ridgway
Carol Bentley • Rachel Gough

Contents

Incredible journeys

This chapter is about people going on journeys or living through dramatic circumstances in far away places. The people in the texts face a range of incredible experiences from the threat of cannon fire to the danger of crocodiles – and the emotions they feel range from absolute fear to extreme joy.

Speaking and listening

1 What different reasons can you think of for why people go on journeys?

2 Choose two famous people who have gone on journeys or expeditions. They can be real or fictional. Explain what they did and why they did it.

3 Describe a memorable journey of your own. Why does it stick in your mind?

1.1 Recounting the past

Hope Leaves Jamaica

The following extract is from a novel by Elizabeth Ernest. It is about Hope, her brother Joshua and her sister Ruth. They are brought up by their grandparents, while their parents go to England to start a new life. In this chapter, Hope's mother and father have just written to request that the children join them in London. Hope has lived all her life in Jamaica.

As you read

Think about:

● the relationship between Hope, Joshua and Ruth and their grandparents. What are the grandparents' expectations of the children?

● the community's reaction to the children leaving.

Hope leaves Jamaica

'Children, your days in the country are numbered,' Grandpa said. He had stopped at the post office. There was a letter from our parents. They had finally booked our air tickets. We were to fly to England in three months' time.

Grandma disappeared into the sitting-room. She returned and handed Grandpa a glass of rum punch. The kitten miaowed and purred as Grandma said slowly, 'Children, you have a baby sister in England.'

'That's impossible,' I said. 'Where did she come from?'

'Just think, you'll be with your parents at last,' Grandma said, hoarsely, ignoring my question. 'Isn't that good news?'

'How can it be good news?' Ruth asked. 'We are leaving you and Grandpa.'

'I asked my teacher to show me England on the map months ago,' Joshua said. 'I wanted to see where Mother and Father lived. Grandpa, you should have told me the truth. I would have understood.' Then he said, 'I don't want to go, Grandpa. I want to stay here with you and Grandma for ever!'

'We'll always be here for you, Joshua,' Grandpa said. 'We never told you that your parents were abroad, because we didn't want you to fret too much.'

'I see,' Joshua said, stroking Jemima without enthusiasm.

I remembered my promise to Cousin Archie: no tears or tantrums when it was time to leave my grandparents. Of course, there would be no tantrums, but I couldn't stop the tears from flowing. I was devastated!

The weeks ahead passed in confusion. We were escorted to Kingston several times. We had to have passports as well as a thorough medical check-up. Meantime, the news spread throughout the village, for Grandpa had read the letter while standing outside the post office. But the villagers were tactful. They never mentioned our impending departure, because they knew that we would break down and weep in public. However, the Sunday school teacher, Miss Violet, presented us with a book of sacred songs, signed by all the children.

The time of our departure drew near and the pastor visited us at home. He said he would miss our obedient faces in church. He blessed us, saying: 'Children, take the name of Jesus with you; He will comfort you always.'

Grandpa said the pastor was not so bad after all. He had prayed with us at home to spare Grandma the anguish of singing at another farewell service.

Uncle Ely and Aunt Esmé also came to see us. They said, sadly, 'Give Robin our love and God go with you.'

Aunt Enid arrived crying. She said, 'Children, Jehovah will guide you over the ocean.' She had received a letter from her son Samuel. He was coming home on vacation.

On our last day at school, the headmaster organised a special assembly. The children crowded round Ruth and Joshua, trying to touch their hands and faces, saying: 'Give Robin Redbreast our love and don't forget your old friends!'

In the assembly hall, the older children sang: 'The day thou gavest, Lord, is ended . . .', 'Land of our birth we pledge to Thee, our love and toil in the years to be . . .', followed by 'Now the day is over, Night is drawing nigh . . .'

When the singing ended, Mr Trelawny said: 'Children, you are marching on from childhood towards the blessed sunny slopes of life; seize opportunity by the hand, so that one day you can return to Jamaica as successful adults.'

I could not imagine leaving Jamaica, let alone returning as an adult. I wanted to be a child for ever. Just then the younger children began to sing 'My Bonny lies over the ocean'.

Parents who lived near the school had come to the assembly – many were in tears. We brought tears to a lot of eyes for we were well known in the surrounding villages, because Grandma and Grandpa had lots of distant relatives.

The farewell ended. A horn sounded at the school gate. We walked down the steps, which no longer seemed scary. I was sad and Miss Clover walked me to the gate,

saying: 'Hope, may your life be happy and all your days be bright . . .'

My eyes filled up with tears and when I opened my mouth to speak, the words just stuck in my throat.

'Grandpa, Grandpa.' Joshua went running. Ruth followed him and they shouted, 'Grandpa has come to collect us!'

In the past, we had begged Grandpa to collect us from school, but he was too busy on the farm. Today was exceptional. He stood by the bakery van with the words United Bakeries written on the side. He opened his arms and Ruth and Joshua flung themselves on to him.

The driver, Mr Brown, opened the sliding door, smiling. He had lost all his hair now. His gold tooth glistened in the sun as he handed us each a small paper bag. The children banged on the side of the van as we slowly moved off, eating freshly baked Jamaican buns.

Next day, we walked around the farm, saying goodbye to the animals. It was as if we had always lived there, because now we could not remember the day we had first arrived when Father had left us. Toby whimpered and we clung to him. Cheyenne neighed and Ruth and Joshua patted him, but I would still not go near him. Dominic and her brood were scratching near the coop. She sensed that something was wrong, for she flew on top of the coop and there she stood clucking, with her small eyes opening and closing. Then Joshua refused to part with Jemima, so Grandpa had to prize her away and she was given to Aunt Esmé.

Uncle Ely was the only man in the village with a car. We squeezed into the Austin Cambridge, stopping in the village square where we got out, trembling with excitement and fear.

A group of farmers rode past, saying: 'Children, we don't envy you, for this time tomorrow you'll be shivering!'

Man-Man and Big-Man appeared with Jubal. But our grandparents remained in the car. The villagers said goodbye to us while Grandpa stared ahead, ignoring Jubal, so he was led back to the corral by Man-Man and Big-Man.

We left the village behind, travelling up the winding mountain road, which no longer terrified us. We stared down at huge boulders of rocks, trembling ferns, burnt-out vehicles in the ravines and the ancient trees that spread their branches like canopies. We silently took it all in and a new dread took hold of us: England!

The road led downward and the countryside was behind us. Finally, we crossed the famous Flat Bridge, in the parish of St Catherine, and Grandpa stared at the Rio Cobre river, saying, 'Rhoda, we're crossing that bridge at last.'

Grandma sniffed while Joshua said: 'Don't worry, Grandpa. When I'm a big man, I'm coming back to help you on the farm.'

'When I grow up,' Ruth said, 'I'm going to be the headmistress of my old school.'

'Anything is possible.' Grandma blew her nose. 'You are going to the land of opportunity.'

Uncle Ely was silent throughout. He was probably thinking about the same journey that he'd made with Robin. When we reached the airport, Grandma produced three handkerchiefs.

'Those are Father's handkerchiefs.' Ruth narrowed her eyes in confusion. 'I thought I had lost them.'

'I put them away for safe keeping,' Grandma said, handing us each a handkerchief. 'I want you children to wave them when you reach the top step of the aeroplane.'

'Children,' Grandpa said, 'this is the last time I'm going to advise you: "labour for learning before you grow old, for learning is better than silver and gold".'

'Your grandpa is right,' Grandma said, smiling. Then she added, 'Children, never forget: "silver and gold will vanish away, but a good education will never decay".'

All the children who left our village received the same advice from teachers or elders. Nevertheless, the words terrified us, for we knew deep down that our promise had to be fulfilled, otherwise we would be letting down our grandparents. Also, we had said too many goodbyes and now words failed us.

Grandpa spoke again: 'Children, there is nothing more for us to give you, except our love. That you know you will have for ever.' Then he and Grandma hugged us really hard.

I felt like a miniature adult when Uncle Ely shook my hand and said: 'Hope, be good and look after the children.'

When we reached the top step of the aeroplane, we stood waving along with many others, though we couldn't see our grandparents. We boarded the aeroplane with tears streaming. Poor Joshua could hardly walk; his legs were trembling so badly. Ruth sobbed into her handkerchief while a yellow-haired stewardess fastened our seat belts and moved off.

The aeroplane sped down the runway. It zoomed upwards and I braced myself, staring down at the blue Caribbean Sea. Meantime, Ruth and Joshua shook with fear. I pleated the handkerchief, thinking, Hope, stop acting like a cry baby. So I dried my eyes and thought about my parents and our life ahead. Then I said to myself, 'We're going to be together at last, but what will the future hold?'

Reading for meaning

1 What is the dramatic news at the beginning of the extract?

2 How do the children react? Is this how you would react in their place?

3 What kind of community do the children live in? How is it described? Use quotations to support your answers.

4 The extract ends with a question. What is the effect of this? There is a name for this literary device. What is it?

5 How does the writer build up the sense of emotion and sadness in this extract? Which nouns, verbs and adjectives help to create this effect?

6 How do you think Hope will find her new life? What differences and problems might she find? What advantages might the family have?

Vocabulary and spelling

This story is set in Jamaica. Do you get any clues in the language that this is the case? Look at:

- people's names

- the description of the landscape.

> A **suffix** is a collection of letters that is added at the end of a baseword. For example: **–full –ment** and **–ure** in 'successful', 'excitement' and 'departure'.

2 Many words with **suffixes** are used in this chapter. Collect your own examples of the suffixes '–ful', '–ment', '–ure'.

> A **synonym** is a word which has the same meaning as another word. For example: 'pastor' and 'vicar'.

3 What other **synonyms** can you think of for 'pastor'? Are they exactly the same as 'pastor' or do they have slightly different meanings?

4 Keep a record of spellings in a spelling log, like the one below.

- Decide first how you want to organise your spelling log – alphabetically or by subject.

- Decide which strategies you will use to remember each word. You can write down a spelling rule, or sound out the word into syllables or note a part of the word you find hard to remember. For example:

Word	Strategies
devastated	1. Word within a word: deva**stated** 2. Sound it out 'de-vast-at-ed'

Speaking and listening

In a group of three, prepare a role-play. Imagine Hope wants to stay in Jamaica, Joshua wants to join his parents in England and Ruth is undecided. Improvise their conversation and present it to the class.

Writing to imagine, explore and entertain

1   You have just read the last chapter of the book 'Hope Leaves Jamaica'. Imagine you have to write the next chapter, which describes Hope getting off the plane and arriving in England.

- Where does she go and what happens?

- How does she feel?

- Decide which characters from the extract will appear and how you will describe them.

Plan your story using a flowchart.

2   a)   After Hope has been in England for a few weeks, she writes a postcard to her grandparents. Look back at the text and think about Hope's relationship with her grandparents.

b)   Now write a postcard to Hope's best friend. How will this postcard be different?

Zlata's Diary

'Zlata's Diary' was written by Zlata Filipovic. She lived in Sarajevo, formerly Yugoslavia, now Bosnia. She began her diary in November 1991; little did she know then that by April of the following year, the country she lived in would be torn apart by war. This extract is taken from a dramatic point of the book when the war is disrupting everybody's lives. She calls her diary 'Mimmy'.

Before you read

1 Have you ever written a diary?

2 Do you know any famous diaries that have been written either recently or long ago? Are they all factual or are some fiction?

3 Why do you think Zlata writes a diary?

Reading for meaning

1 What happened at Zlata's aunt's house? Pick at least one quotation to support your answer.

2 What has happened to Zlata's mother's Uncle Halim? What is Zlata implying when she writes: 'this war speeded up his death'?

3 What are the positive and negative aspects of the war from Zlata's point of view?

- You may wish to use the following headings:

Negative aspects	Positive aspects
Bombs falling near Zlata's flat	Playing with cat Cici

- Use short quotations to support your points.

4 How does the health of Zlata's father affect the rest of the family? Which things we may take for granted do not work in Sarajevo?

Zlata's Diary

Tuesday, 4 August 1992

Dear Mimmy,

Five months. Five months of brutal aggression against the independent, sovereign state of Bosnia and Herzegovina.
A bullet entered the Bobars' sitting room. It shattered the window, broke the TV aerial and part of the glass table, went through the armchair, broke the glass on the door, and finally FELL! The Bobars have had three other bullets. One tore through the plastic and lodged sideways in the wardrobe where it grazed Auntie Boda's university diploma and, finally, FELL! Another one broke through a window and lodged in the wall. And the third ripped through the plastic, grazed the armchair, entered Auntie Boda's closet where it tore her vest and then again – FELL!

Wednesday, 5 August 1992

Dear Mimmy,

Another sad piece of news in the paper. Mummy found out that her uncle (Uncle Halim) has died. He was old but this war speeded up his death. I'm so sorry. He was a wonderful old man. I loved him. That's how it is in wartime, Mimmy. Your loved ones die and you don't even know about it. War doesn't let you stay in touch with people, except for your neighbours. The neighbourhood is our life now. Everything happens within that circle, it's the circle you know, everything else is remote.
Zlata

Friday, 7 August 1992

Dear Mimmy,

It thundered here today. I don't know how many shells fell near by. It was quiet when Daddy went with Samra to get the aid package. But then the shelling suddenly started. An explosion. It thundered. Emina was at our place. There was a terrible boom. Glass shattered, bricks fell, there were clouds of dust. We didn't know where to run. We were convinced that the shell had fallen on our roof. We were on our way to the cellar when we heard Nedo frantically calling out to us, running towards us through the dust, bricks and broken glass. We ran over to the Bobars' cellar. They were all down there. We were shaking. Mummy most of all. In tears, she asked about Daddy, whether he had come back. When we calmed down a bit they told us that a shell had fallen on the roof of Emina's house, above her flat. We were lucky, because that's only about ten metres away from the roof over our flat. Everything turned out OK. Daddy and Samra soon came running in. They had been worried about us too. When we got back to the flat it was full of dust, pieces of brick, and we found a piece of shrapnel in the bathroom. We rolled up our sleeves and started cleaning the place up. I was scared it would start again. Luckily, it didn't. Another horrible day.
Your Zlata

Monday, 10 August 1992

Dear Mimmy,

Mummy's Braco is fine. He's already walking well. Today he went to Otes. He'll be working in the press centre there, reporting on the situation. Things are all right there. They have no shooting and they have food. They're lucky. I really miss my cousins Mikica and Daèa. I haven't seen them since the war broke out.
Your Zlata

Tuesday, 11 August 1992

Dear Mimmy,

Shelling, killing, darkness and hunger continue in Sarajevo. Sad!
I still don't go out. I play with Bojana and with my kitty Cici. Cici
has brightened up this misery of a life. How you can come to love
an animal! She doesn't talk, but she speaks with her eyes, her paws,
her meows, and I understand her. I really love you, Cici.
Ciao!
Zlata

Friday, 14 August 1992

Dear Mimmy,

Last night the Bobars came to listen to RFI, the way they do every
night. Bojana and I were playing cards. We were all relaxed
somehow and forgot for a moment that we are living in a war. The
shelling started at around 21.30. Out of the blue, the way it usually
does. We raced over to Nedo's place. The shooting died down
around midnight and we returned home. You can't relax for even a
second!
Zlata

Sunday, 16 August 1992

Dear Mimmy,

Daddy has a hernia. He's lost a lot of weight and carrying the water
was too much for him. The doctor has told him that he mustn't lift
anything heavy any more. Mustn't? But somebody has to bring the
water! Mummy will have to do it alone now. How will she
manage?
Zlata

Tuesday, 18 August 1992

Dear Mimmy,

Mummy is carrying home the water. It's hard on her, but she has to do it. The water hasn't come back on. Nor has the electricity. I didn't tell you, Mimmy, but I've forgotten what it's like to have water pouring out of a tap, what it's like to shower. We use a jug now. The jug has replaced the shower. We wash dishes and clothes like in the Middle Ages. This war is taking us back to olden times. And we take it, we suffer it, but we don't know for how long. Zlata

Friday, 21 August 1992

Dear Mimmy,

I'm not in any of the classes I thought I'd be in at summer school. I've signed up for the literature and drama club. They gave me Abdulah Sidran's 'Sarajevo Prayer' to recite. It's great. Zlata

Tuesday, 25 August 1992

Dear Mimmy,

I go regularly to summer school. I like it. We're together. We don't think about the shelling or the war. Maja and Lela, who help our teacher Irena Vidovic, cheer us up. We write, we recite, we spend the hours together. It takes me back to the days before the war. I'm also glad to be able to go out into the street. True, it's not far away (200 metres from my house), but I've finally stepped outside. Daddy takes me. Children mustn't walk in the street alone in Sarajevo. I was already going stir-crazy. And I 'do myself up', I wear something nice. I mustn't show off too much. Ciao! Zlata

Saturday, 29 August 1992

Dear Mimmy,

I'm feeling good today. There's no shooting, I go to summer school, play with Maja, Bojana and Nedo. We fool around, we have our own kind of humour. Sometimes we laugh so much we even forget about the war. We simply get carried away and it's peace time again. But only until something bursts or explodes. Then we come back to reality. Sometimes I think that if it weren't for them I don't know how I'd be able to stand it. Thank you Maja, Bojana and Nedo, for making it easier for me to take everything that's happening, for killing my boredom and my thoughts about all these ugly things.

Remember them, Mimmy, don't ever forget them. I certainly won't.

Your Zlata

Thursday, 3 September 1992

Dear Mimmy,

The days are passing by more pleasantly. There's no shooting in our neighbourhood, but we've been without electricity now for more than a month. If only the electricity would come back on. If only I could cross the bridge and at least go to Grandma's and Grandad's! I'm working on it. I'm putting pressure on Mummy and Daddy. Will it work???? We'll find out!

Zlata

Tuesday, 8 September 1992

Dear Mimmy,

YESS! YESS! YESS! THE ELECTRICITY IS BACK!!!!!!

Tomorrow is Mummy's birthday. I made a paper heart and wrote HAPPY BIRTHDAY on it . . . and I cut a bouquet of roses out of the newspaper.

Mummy started making a cake, the kind you don't need to cook, and when everything was finished, the electricity came back on . . . OOOHHHH!!!!!!!

Your Zlata

Vocabulary, punctuation and sentences

A **verb** is the word in the sentence that describes what a person or object is doing. For example:

'The bullet **shattered** the window.' Zlata has used some vivid verbs to add atmosphere to her writing.

1   Look at the diary entry for 7 August. This is a dramatic piece of writing. Pick out **verbs** that add to the drama of the description of the bombs falling and the effect on the people involved.

2   a) Look up the word 'shrapnel' in a dictionary. What is the origin of this word?

   b) Find five other words associated with war in the extract.

Zlata uses a variety of sentence lengths. In this extract, the sentences which are short give a real sense of drama and anxiety. The longer sentences then fill in the details. For example:

'We were shaking. Mummy most of all. In tears, she asked about Daddy, whether he had come back. When we calmed down a bit they told us that a shell had fallen on the roof of Emina's house, above her flat.'

3   Choose another diary entry. Look at the length of the sentences Zlata uses. How does Zlata's use of different sentence types affect meaning?

Writing to inform, explain and describe

1   Imagine that Zlata's mother or father is also keeping a diary. Choose two diary entries and write them from their point of view.

   • Choose vocabulary carefully and think about using a more adult tone.

   • Think of how they would react to the same situations as Zlata. For example: baking the birthday cake (mother), not being able to carry the water (father).

2   Zlata became a famous personality while she was writing this diary. Imagine you are given the chance to interview Zlata for your school magazine. Write the script of your interview with Zlata.

   Before you start, think of some really searching questions which would elicit interesting answers. Use open questions, rather than closed questions with 'yes' and 'no' answers.

1.2 Dangerous adventures

The Wonderful Adventures of Mary Seacole

The Crimean War was fought between Russia and an alliance of Britain, France, Turkey and Sardinia. Russian aggression against Turkey led to war in 1853. British and French troops eventually captured the fortress city of Sebastopol in 1855. This led to the signing of a peace treaty in 1856.

Mary Seacole was a nurse, cook and hotel keeper whose bravery made her very famous during her lifetime. She stayed on the front line during the Crimean War, facing many dangers while she nursed the soldiers of the British army.

This extract is written about the final stages of the war in 1856, during the siege of Sebastopol.

As you read

The Crimean War was fought before the introduction of tanks and modern warfare. Medical provision was very poor. The war was conducted on the ground and in trenches. As you read, think about Mary Seacole's decision to work on the front line, her character and her motivation.

The Wonderful Adventures of Mary Seacole

The bombardment of Sebastopol

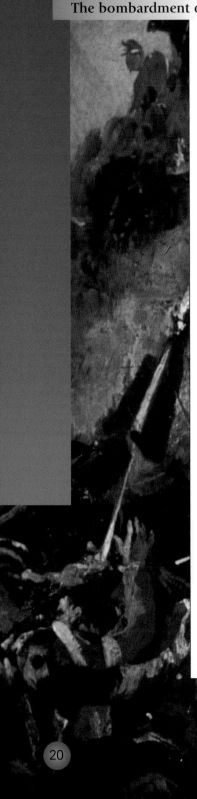

The three weeks following the battle of the Tchernaya were, I should think, some of the busiest and most eventful the world has ever seen. There was little doing at Spring Hill[1]. Every one was either at his post, or too anxiously awaiting the issue of the last great bombardment to spend much time at the British Hotel. I think that I lost more of my patients and customers during those few weeks than during the whole previous progress of the siege. Scarcely a night passed that I was not lulled to sleep with the heavy continuous roar of the artillery, scarce a morning dawned that the same sound did not usher in my day's work. The ear grew so accustomed during those weeks to the terrible roar, that when Sebastopol fell the sudden quiet seemed unnatural and made us dull.

During the whole of this time the most perplexing rumours flew about, some having reference to the day of assault, the majority relative to the last great effort which it was supposed the Russians would make to drive us into the sea. I confess these latter rumours now and then caused me temporary uneasiness, Spring Hill being on the direct line of route which the actors in such a tragedy must take.

I spent much of my time on Cathcart's Hill, watching with a curiosity and excitement which became intense, the progress of the terrible bombardment[2]. Now and then a shell would fall among the crowd of onlookers which covered the hill but it never disturbed us, so keen and feverish and so deadened to danger had the excitement and expectation made us.

---

1 Mary Seacole set up and ran the British Hotel for officers and soldiers at Spring Hill. She used this as a base from which to nurse the wounded.

2 The French and British were bombarding Sebastopol which was under siege. This would have been visible from Cathcart's Hill.

The ceremony of the Order of the Bath[1]

In the midst of the bombardment took place the important ceremony of distributing the Order of the Bath to those selected for that honour. I contrived to witness this ceremony very pleasantly and, although it cost me a day, I considered that I had fairly earned the pleasure. I was anxious to have some personal share in the affair, so I made and forwarded to headquarters, a cake which Gunter might have been at some loss to manufacture with the materials at my command and which I adorned gaily with banners, flags, etc. I received great kindness from the officials at the ceremony and from the officers— some of rank—who recognised me, indeed, I held quite a little *levée* around my chair.

The closing days

Well, a few days after this ceremony, I thought the end of the world, instead of the war, was at hand, when every battery opened and poured a perfect hail of shot and shell upon the beautiful city which I had left the night before sleeping so calm and peaceful beneath the stars. The firing began at early dawn and was fearful. Sleep was impossible, so I arose and set out for my old station on Cathcart's Hill. And here, with refreshments for the anxious onlookers, I spent most of my time, right glad of any excuse to witness the last scene of the siege. It was from this spot that I saw fire after fire break out in Sebastopol and watched all night the beautiful yet terrible effect of a great ship blazing in the harbour and lighting up the adjoining country for miles.

The 8th of September[2]

The weather changed, as it often did in the Crimea, most capriciously and the morning of the memorable 8th of September broke cold and wintry. The same little bird which had let me into so many secrets, also gave me a hint of what this day was pregnant with and very early in the morning I was on horseback, with my bandages and refreshments ready to repeat the work of the 18th of June last. A line of sentries forbade all strangers passing through without orders,

---

1 The Order of the Bath was a ceremony used to knight someone.

2 The 8th of September was critical in the progress of the recapture of Sebastopol. It was the day that the Malakhoff fortress fell.

even to Cathcart's Hill, but once more I found that my reputation served as a permit and the officers relaxed the rule in my favour everywhere. So, early in the day, I was in my old spot, with my old appliances for the wounded and fatigued, little expecting however, that this day would so closely resemble the day of the last attack in its disastrous results.

French troops make the final advance

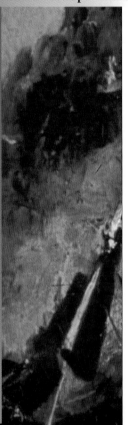

It was noon before the cannonading suddenly ceased and we saw, with a strange feeling of excitement, the French tumble out of their advanced trenches and roll into the Malakhoff like a human flood. Onward they seemed to go into the dust and smoke, swallowed up by hundreds, but they never returned and before long we saw workmen levelling parapets and filling up ditches, over which they drove, with headlong speed and impetuosity, artillery and ammunition wagons, until there could be no doubt that the Malakhoff was taken, although the tide of battle still surged around it with violence and wounded men being borne from it in large numbers. Before this, our men had made their attack and the fearful assault of the Redan was going on and failing. But I was soon too busy to see much for the wounded were brought to me in even greater numbers than at the last assault, whilst stragglers, slightly hurt, limped in, in fast-increasing numbers, and engrossed our attention. I now and then found time to ask them rapid questions, but they did not appear to know anything more than that everything had gone wrong. The sailors, as before, showed their gallantry and even recklessness, conspicuously. The wounded of the ladder and sandbag parties came up even with a laugh and joked about their hurts in the happiest possible manner.

Treating the wounded

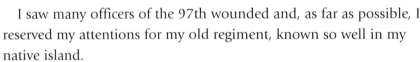

I saw many officers of the 97th wounded and, as far as possible, I reserved my attentions for my old regiment, known so well in my native island.

My poor 97th, their loss was terrible. I dressed the wound of one of its officers, seriously hit in the mouth. I attended to another wounded in the throat and bandaged the hand of a third terribly crushed by a rifle bullet. In the midst of this we were often interrupted by those unwelcome and impartial Russian visitors—the shells. One fell so near that I thought my last hour was come and, although I had sufficient firmness to throw myself upon the ground, I was so seriously frightened that I never thought of rising from my recumbent position until the hearty laugh of those around convinced me that the danger had passed by. Afterwards I picked up a piece of this huge shell and brought it home with me

It was on this, as on every similar occasion, that I saw *The Times* correspondent eagerly taking down notes and sketches of the scene, under fire—listening apparently with attention to all the busy little crowd that surrounded him, but without laying down his pencil and yet finding time, even in his busiest moment, to lend a helping hand to the wounded. It may have been on this occasion that his keen eye noticed me and his mind, albeit engrossed with far more important memories, found room to remember me. I may well be proud of his testimony, borne so generously only the other day and may well be excused for transcribing it from the columns of *The Times*:

> *I have seen her go down, under fire, with her little store of creature comforts for our wounded men and a more tender or skilful hand about a wound or broken limb could not be found among our best surgeons. I saw her at the assault on the Redan, at the Tchernaya, at the fall of Sebastopol, laden, not with plunder (good old soul), but with wine, bandages and food for the wounded or the prisoners.*

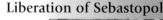

Liberation of Sebastopol

I remained on Cathcart's Hill far into the night and watched the city blazing beneath us, awestruck at the terrible sight, until the bitter wind found its way through my thin clothing and chilled me to the bone. Not till then did I leave.

I had little sleep. The night was made a ruddy lurid day with the glare of the blazing town, while every now and then came reports which shook the earth to its centre. And yet I believe very many of the soldiers, wearied with their day's labour, slept soundly throughout that terrible night and awoke to find their work completed. For in the night, covered by the burning city, Sebastopol was left, a heap of ruins, to its victors and before noon on the following day, none but dead and dying Russians were in the south side of the once famous and beautiful mistress-city of the Euxene.

Reading for meaning

1 In paragraph three, what effect has the shelling had on Mary Seacole?

2 Why does she take some time off and what does she make in paragraph four?

3 Describe some of the things Mary does to help the soldiers. Use quotations to support the points you make.

4 Why do you think Mary included the extract from *The Times* in her memoirs? What does this tell you about her character?

5 What feelings and emotions is Mary trying to convey to the reader in the final paragraph?

Vocabulary

1 a) The language of war is present throughout this extract. Find these words in the passage and use their context to work out a definition. Use a dictionary to look up the precise meanings.

Word	Meaning
Assault	
Artillery	
Bombardment	
Cannonading	
Reports	
Trenches	

  b) Look through the text and pick out five examples of archaic language.

Archaic forms of language are old and no longer used in modern English. You can sometimes tell how old a text is by the archaic words and sentences used.

2 There are some words and phrases which have changed in meaning over the years since Mary Seacole wrote this book. What do you think the following phrases mean?

a) 'this day was pregnant with'

b) 'sailors … showed their gallantry'

c) 'the night was made a ruddy lurid day'

Research

1 Find out what you can about Mary Seacole. Use some of the following information sources: a learning resources centre; your local library; the Internet.

2 Write a short entry in a biographical dictionary about Mary Seacole's life. You will need to include her full name, date and place of birth, who her parents were (if relevant), her job, what she did to be famous, her interests and concerns, what she wrote, when she died. Your writing should be quite factual and not descriptive.

Writing to inform, explain and describe

Mary Seacole nursed many soldiers in the 97th division. Imagine you are a soldier tended by Mary. Write a letter to someone you know well.

● How will you set out the letter? Use as your address 'The British Hotel, Spring Hill'.

● What details will you concentrate on? Information about the fighting, about Mary, about your injuries, about your comrades?

Reading for meaning

1 a) What were the rumours that Mary refers to in the second paragraph?

b) Why did some of them make her feel uneasy?

2 Why were the onlookers not disturbed by the falling shells in the third paragraph?

3 a) How did Mary get her information on the morning of 8th September?

b) How did she get through the sentries? Why do you think this was?

An African Adventure

In the 1970s, Christina Dodwell answered an advertisement for a travelling companion and went travelling across Africa in a landrover. The adventures described here did not put her off; she has continued to travel far and wide and has written books about journeying though China and other exciting places.

Travel writing is a genre of writing which shows the journey of someone through places away from their home. It is usually written in the **first person**. Sometimes the person writes while on the journey, sometimes when they return to their own country. Travel writing is often written in an exciting and pacy way, describing adventures, characters and different cultures which are experienced by the writer. There is often some reflection on all of these elements, comparing them to the writer's experiences at home.

As you read

Think about:

- what difficulties the two women face on the river
- how they overcome their problems.

An African Adventure

We drifted and paddled leisurely onwards, ran up against a submerged sandbank, climbed out and pushed, glided on, then hit another sandbank, climbed out and pushed again, but every inch only wedged the dugout tighter and higher on the sand. Soon it was stuck firm. The water was only a few inches deep. We pushed and pulled and dug away the sand from underneath, but got nowhere. A strong fisherman paddled up, gave our dugout a hearty shove, refloated it, and handed us another fish.

In a short time, we were out of the sandbanks and onto a fast straight stretch of river. We raced along feeling elated with the wind blowing through our hair as we sped the paddles in short rapid strokes through the water. We zigzagged among the clumps of hyacinth which floated spinning lazily in the swirling movement of the current. Then the surface of the river suddenly erupted and we shot head-on into the bank. The surface of the river could change abruptly; one moment the water would be flowing strongly but placidly, and the next instant it became a raging, bubbling mass of wide circles which spun with uplifted edges. I presumed that they must have been caused by the powerful underwater currents hitting rocks or shoals on the riverbed, and as the current veered to a specific angle, so the surface erupted in turmoil. The local people called them whirlpools. Many were permanent whirlpools, like the ones round every headland, some were small and weak, others were very large and very strong. Being caught in them produced a feeling similar to driving a car on ice; suddenly you were out of control, skidding and sliding weightlessly.

To begin with we were not very good at managing the dugout[1]; we spent a lot of time hurtling downriver broadside or backwards, both shouting instructions to each other that neither could hear. We were growing expert at spreading out our soaked belongings to dry in the sun. The tarpaulin was constantly wet because it lay in the bottom of the dugout, and as soon as we dried it, something unfortunate would happen. Accidents such as once when Lesley was carrying the freshly dried tarpaulin down to *La Pirogue*, which had moved out slightly

---

1 A dugout is a small boat made by cutting out a hollow space in a tree trunk.

from the shore. Lesley took two paces in ankle deep water, and at the third step she fell up to her neck in the river. The tarpaulin was soaked again, and we laughed until we cried.

Nights were less horrifying after Lesley suggested that we try sleeping on the shore in the breeze and not too close to the water's edge. The first night we tried that we found a riverside glade on the Zaire bank and made camp there. Within half an hour three men arrived in a dugout, and one, who claimed he was a member of the militia, came ashore. He wanted to see our papers and examine our boat. We were rather anxious because we didn't have visas for Zaire, but we needn't have worried—he didn't know how to read. After looking intently at the pictures he turned to *La Pirogue*, started pulling all our gear out of the tin trunk and ordered us to tell him what it was for. We knew from experience that if we explained the items then every time he saw something he fancied he would demand it. So we offered him coffee and sat chatting with him instead. He was very pleasant and he left after dark. We dug the tent poles into the ground, draped our mosquito nets over them, and settled down to sleep. The mosquitoes invaded us but it was not as bad as before. Then it started to rain so we got up to pull the tarpaulin over the dugout. The rain was followed by the noise of monkeys fighting, squealing in anger and throwing nuts at each other which landed on us. Finally, there was peace and quiet, except for the eerie howling of a wildcat hunting nearby in the forest.

In the middle of the night the militia man returned. This time it was a social call—he had brought a huge smoked catfish to eat as a midnight feast. It was delicious, but the man showed no signs of going away. I had an inspiration. I started to scratch. I scratched my arms and legs and head as though I was thick with fleas; Lesley joined in. It had a potent psychological effect and after five minutes the militia man bade us goodnight.

Our second visit to Zaire was more fun. We stopped at a village to refill our giant water container, which was almost empty and we found that the local water supply was of course the river. The river was a muddy brown colour from the rains, which were falling here and to the north, but if the villagers could drink it then so could we. A huge crowd had gathered round us the moment we stepped ashore, the atmosphere was friendly, but they stared and stared. The bolder ones spoke to us in simple French and asked if they could touch our hair, exclaiming with wonder at its softness. Others peered curiously at the colour of our skin, assuming that the whiteness was due to a disease. Several people wanted to know if we were girls.

Then they brought out two stools, sat us down, and stared at us for a long time. I was equally curious about them. Most of the people wore grass skirts, and I noticed some remarkable tribal brands, including many narrowly-spaced parallel lines which gave their faces a weird stripy look. At first I felt embarrassed about wanting to stare at Africans, I had always considered it impolite. But in Africa it is not rude to stare and by tradition a newcomer was usually expected to sit or squat while he was scrutinised for half an hour. When the people were satisfied having looked at his appearance, they would formally demand to know his tribe and destination.

"What tribe are you?" asked a big man standing at the front.

"English," I answered.

"Where are you going?"

"To Brazzaville."

A murmur ran through the crowd, and the big man who was obviously their chief observed (in all seriousness) that we would not reach Brazzaville before nightfall, so we had better stay the night in his village.

They were gregarious affable people; they wanted to know about the countries we came from and why we were paddling down the river. Lesley noticed a young girl with some infected sores on her arms and asked if she could help her. Our medical kit consisted only of aspirin, nivaquine and a tube of antibiotic cream, but Lesley couldn't bear to see untreated injuries or people in pain. The girl took us to her parents' hut where we boiled some water and someone brought a piece of cloth to tear into bandages. Then someone else came and requested Lesley to go and look at his sick father, and several people turned up who seemed to have malaria, so Lesley dispensed some nivaquine to them. Quinine was the only cure for malaria; I was surprised to learn that quinine trees did not grow in Africa. For while malaria could be a killer, it seemed that the Africans had adapted to some extent and only suffered from a mild form of it.

A tiny man whose chin only reached to the height of my waist asked in gestures for Lesley to come and attend to someone who had been wounded by an elephant. It was quite a long walk, inland from the river on a small path through the forest which was very overgrown with vines and creeper that wrapped itself round our necks and ankles. Every plant had thorns. Many of the trees had claws like large rose bushes which grew all over their trunks and branches. Other trees had spikes; the vines had thorns, the bushes had barbed prickles, the undergrowth was a tangle of brambles, briars and thistles. The little pygmy man slipped through the forest as though it was silk, but Lesley and I got lassoed, tripped up, and clawed by every plant we passed.

He took us to a pygmy village where huts were simple grass shelters in contrast to the mud and thatch of those of the river tribes. Pygmies seemed to live a hunter-gatherer style of existence, moving from place to place in search of a fresh supply of food. Six pygmies were standing beside one of the shelters, the tallest of them was about four feet high. They weren't dwarfs—but they looked like miniature people. They were wearing loin cloths and a couple had quivers of arrows slung over their shoulders, but all six of them vanished off among the trees when they saw us.

The man who had been hit by the elephant was lying in the shelter; he had a deep gash in one leg, but Lesley said it wasn't serious. He watched her every move as she cleaned and bandaged the wound, and when she finished he smiled and chanted a sing song speech. The forest was quiet. No one was going to return to the settlement while we were there, and since it was probably getting late we hurried back to the river village. The chief welcomed us back, and sat us on stools outside his hut. The crowd gathered to watch what we did. I felt like an animal on display and wished that I could perform tricks for them. My only trick was to fill and smoke my pipe, which startled them as effectively as if I had done a series of cartwheels.

During a supper of hot peppered fish and spinach, I asked the chief about the pygmy tribe. He told me they seldom came to the river (none of the pygmies were river people) and they never inter-married with other tribes. Other tribes considered the pygmies equivalent to animals. He added that we would see a few more of them in the morning because it was market day and they would bring dried antelope to trade in the village. Lesley and I shared a wooden bedstead in our hut; it wasn't sprung but the mattress was made of bundles of rushes and was very comfortable.

The morning market was a good time for us to stock up our food supplies which had dwindled to half a loaf of bread, jam and three maize cobs. It was not a busy market—it was more a village social gathering. We walked around chatting to people as we tried to decide what to buy. There was no need to buy anything because all the villagers came up to say thank you to Lesley for helping their sick families, and they gave us presents of plantain and sweet bananas, maize, smoked fish, cassava and pawpaw in such quantity that the centre section of the dugout was too full for us to move from front to back unless we balanced on all fours and clambered along the rim of the sides. We shook hands with everyone and just as we were casting off the little pygmy man came running down to give us a chunk of antelope. Then we set off and the people lined the bank to wave goodbye.

Reading for meaning

1 List the problems encountered by the women in this extract. How do they respond to each problem?

2 Who do the travellers meet on their journey? How do the two travellers communicate with the people they meet?

3 Look at the first sentence in the paragraph beginning 'the man who had been hit by the elephant…'. How does Christina Dodwell involve you by her use of a short sentence in the middle of the paragraph?

4 Would you like to go on a journey like this? Why?

Vocabulary and spelling

1 Christina Dodwell uses some very vivid language. Look up the following words and check you know their meanings: 'tarpaulin', 'cassava', 'elated', 'placidly', 'militia', 'scrutinised'. *Hint: Your guess might be a better definition than the dictionary definition.*

2 Write your answers in table form, like the one shown here.

Word	Meaning in context (guess)	Definition in dictionary	Spelling strategy
tarpaulin			
cassava			
elated			
placidly			
militia			
scrutinised			

Speaking and listening

1   Group A. You are a travel company called Adventure Quest that organises group travel for young people. Prepare a presentation to persuade pupils and teachers to go on an adventure such as the one described in 'An African Adventure'.

You may use the following headings to help you:

Benefits of travelling:
- experiencing new ideas
- facing mental and physical challenges
- seeing different landscapes

You will also have to overcome the potential worries people might have concerning physical dangers and disease.

2   Group B. You are a group of school students. You want to go on a group adventure to Africa with a company called Adventure Quest. You need to persuade a sponsor to give you money which will enable you to go on this journey.

The sponsor is a company that produces adventure gear, clothing and equipment. You will need to convince them of the educational value of the trip, and offer to record your adventure in some way so they can use your experience for publicity.

South

During an unsuccessful expedition to the South Pole in 1914, Ernest Shackleton's ship 'The Endurance' was destroyed by pack ice. He and his crew then had to make the dangerous journey home on a small ship called *The Caird*. In this extract, the crew are travelling from Elephant Island to South Georgia in a desperate attempt to reach civilisation. They are suffering from exhaustion and extreme thirst. Shackleton's account describes all the drama of their situation, from dreadful danger to success, sometimes in a matter of minutes.

Before you read

1 Which famous explorers do you know who have experienced extremely cold climates either now or in the past?

2 What problems would explorers have in the 1900s which we could overcome today?

3 What **nautical** terms do you know? Shackleton was a sailor and used many technical words relating to sailing.

Nautical is an adjective connected with ships, sailing and the sea.

South

Thirst took possession of us. I dared not permit the allowance of water to be increased since an unfavourable wind might drive us away from the island and lengthen our voyage by many days. Lack of water is always the most severe privation that men can be condemned to endure, and we found, as during our earlier boat voyage, that the salt water in our clothing and the salt spray that lashed our faces made our thirst grow quickly to a burning pain. I had to be very firm in refusing to allow any one to anticipate the morrow's allowance, which I was sometimes begged to do. We did the necessary work dully and hoped for the land. I had altered the course to the east so as to make sure of our striking the island, which would have been impossible to regain if we had run past the northern end. The course was laid on our scrap of chart for a point some thirty miles down the coast.

That day and the following day passed for us in a sort of nightmare. Our mouths were dry and our tongues were swollen. The wind was still strong and the heavy sea forced us to navigate carefully, but any thought of our peril from the waves was buried beneath the consciousness of our raging thirst. The bright moments were those when we each received our one mug of hot milk during the long, bitter watches of the night. Things were bad for us in those days, but the end was coming. The morning of May 8 broke thick and stormy, with squalls from the north-west. We searched the waters ahead for a sign of land, and though we could see nothing more than had met our eyes for many days, we were cheered by a sense that the goal was near at hand. About ten o'clock that morning we passed a little bit of kelp, a glad signal of the proximity of land. An hour later we saw two shags sitting on a big mass of kelp, and knew then that we must be within ten or fifteen miles of the shore. These birds are as sure an indication of the proximity of land as a lighthouse is, for they never venture far to sea. We gazed ahead with increasing eagerness, and at 12.30 p.m., through a rift in the clouds, McCarthy caught a glimpse of the black cliffs of South Georgia, just fourteen days after our departure from Elephant Island. It was a glad moment. Thirst-ridden, chilled, and weak as we were, happiness irradiated us. The job was nearly done.

We stood in towards the shore to look for a landing-place, and presently we could see the green tussock-grass on the ledges above the surf-beaten rocks. Ahead of us and to the south, blind rollers showed the presence of uncharted reefs along the coast. Here and there the hungry rocks were close to the surface, and over them the great waves broke, swirling viciously and spouting thirty and forty feet into the air. The rocky coast appeared to descend sheer to the sea. Our need of water and rest was well-nigh desperate, but to have attempted a landing at that time would have been suicidal. Night was drawing near, and the weather indications were not favourable. There was nothing for it but to haul off till the following morning, so we stood away on the starboard tack until we had made what appeared to be a safe offing. Then we hove to in the high westerly swell. The hours passed slowly as we awaited the dawn, which would herald, we fondly hoped, the last stage of our journey. Our thirst was a torment and we could scarcely touch our food; the cold seemed to strike right through our weakened bodies. At 5 a.m. the wind shifted to the north-west and quickly increased to one of the worst hurricanes any of us had ever experienced. A great cross-sea was running, and the wind simply shrieked as it tore the tops off the waves and converted the whole seascape into a haze of driving spray. Down into valleys, up to tossing heights, straining until her seams opened, swung our little boat, brave still but labouring heavily. We knew that the wind and set of the sea was driving us ashore, but we could do nothing. The dawn showed us a storm-torn ocean, and the morning passed without bringing us a sight of the land; but at 1 p.m., through a rift in the flying mists, we got a glimpse of the huge crags of the island and realized that our position had become desperate. We were on a dead lee shore, and we could gauge our approach to the unseen cliffs by the roar of the breakers against the sheer walls of rock. I ordered the double-reefed mainsail to be set in the hope that we might claw off, and this attempt increased the strain upon the boat.

The *Caird* was bumping heavily, and the water was pouring in everywhere. Our thirst was forgotten in the realisation of our imminent danger, as we baled unceasingly, and adjusted our weights from time to time; occasional glimpses showed that the shore was nearer. I knew that Annewkow Island lay to the south of us, but our small and badly marked chart showed uncertain reefs in the passage between the island and the mainland, and I dared not trust it, though as a last resort we could try to lie under the lee of the island. The afternoon wore away as we edged down the coast, with the thunder of the breakers in our ears. The approach of evening found us still some distance from Annewkow Island, and, dimly in the twilight, we could see a snow-capped mountain looming above us. The chance of surviving the night, with the driving gale and the implacable sea forcing us on to the lee shore, seemed small. I think most of us had a feeling that the end was very near. Just after 6 p.m., in the dark, as the boat was in the yeasty backwash from the seas flung from this iron-bound coast, then, just when things looked their worst, they changed for the best. I have marvelled often at the thin line that divides success from failure and the sudden turn that leads from apparently certain disaster to comparative safety. The wind suddenly shifted, and we were free once more to make an offing. Almost as soon as the gale eased, the pin that locked the mast to the thwart fell out. It must have been on the point of doing this throughout the hurricane, and if it had gone nothing could have saved us; the mast would have snapped like a carrot. Our backstays had carried away once before when iced up and were not too strongly fastened now. We were thankful indeed for the mercy that had held that pin in its place throughout the hurricane.

We stood off shore again, tired almost to the point of apathy. Our water had long been finished. The last was about a pint of hairy liquid, which we strained through a bit of gauze from the medicine-chest. The pangs of thirst attacked us with redoubled intensity, and I felt that we must make a landing on the following day at almost any hazard.

The night wore on. We were very tired. We longed for day.

When at last the dawn came on the morning of May 10 there was practically no wind, but a high cross sea was running. We made slow progress towards the shore. About 8 a.m. the wind backed to the north-west and threatened another blow. We had sighted in the meantime a big indentation which I thought must be King Haakon Bay, and I decided that we must land there. We set the bows of the boat towards the bay and ran before the freshening gale. Soon we had angry reefs on either side. Great glaciers came down to the sea and offered no landing-place. The sea spouted on the reefs and thundered against the shore. About noon we sighted a line of jagged reef, like blackened teeth, that seemed to bar the entrance to the bay. Inside, comparatively smooth water stretched eight or nine miles to the head of the bay. A gap in the reef appeared, and we made for it. But the fates had another rebuff for us.

The wind shifted and blew from the east right out of the bay. We could see the way through the reef, but we could not approach it directly. That afternoon we bore up, tacking five times in the strong wind. The last tack enabled us to get through, and at last we were in the wide mouth of the bay. Dusk was approaching. A small cove, with a boulder-strewn beach guarded by a reef, made a break in the cliffs on the south side of the bay, and we turned in that direction. I stood in the bows directing the steering as we ran through the kelp and made the passage of the reef. The entrance was so narrow that we had to take in the oars, and the swell was piling itself right over the reef into the cove; but in a minute or two we were inside, and in the gathering darkness the *James Caird* ran in on a swell and touched the beach. I sprang ashore with the short painter and held on when the boat went out with the backward surge. When the *James Caird* came in again three of the men got ashore, and they held the painter while I climbed some rocks with another line.

A slip on the wet rocks twenty feet up nearly closed my part of the story just at the moment when we were achieving safety. A jagged piece of rock held me and at the same time bruised me sorely. However, I made fast the line, and in a few minutes we were all safe on the beach, with the boat floating in the surging water just off the shore. We heard a gurgling sound that was sweet music in our ears, and, peering around, found a stream of fresh water almost at our feet. A moment later we were down on our knees drinking the pure ice-cold water in long draughts that put new life into us. It was a splendid moment.

Reading for meaning

1 a) Look through the text again and list all the problems encountered by Shackleton and his crew.

   b) Say how each problem was resolved.

2 Look at the first paragraph. How does Shackleton convey the extreme thirst his sailors are experiencing? *Hint: Look at sentence length and choice of words.*

3 How is the sea described throughout this extract? Can you pick out any examples of **personification**?

> **Personification** is a literary technique in which an object (in this case the sea) is described as having human qualities. For example: Shackleton uses personification to describe the violence of the sea – *angry* reefs and *shrieking* winds. This adds to the drama of the situation.

Writing to inform, explain and describe

1 Once Shackleton and his crew had landed their boat and set up camp, Shackleton and Worsley decided to leave the crew and try to cross the island to get help. You are one of the other sailors. Write to a family member or friend about this part of your dangerous journey. You give the letter to Shackleton to post if he finds civilisation. Think about:

   ● your emotional state and your physical state – will you say how much you have suffered?

   ● the journey – describe the sea dramatically.

2 Imagine you are a newspaper journalist. You are given a copy of the letter from exercise 1 from a member of Shackleton's crew. You decide to use it to write a newspaper report.

   ● Think of a suitable headline.

   ● Plan your report carefully, try to answer questions of what, where, when, why and how things happened.

1.3 Poetry

The Listeners

Not every traveller knows where he is going or why. The following poem by Walter de la Mare is full of mystery and unanswered questions. A man dismounts from his horse and approaches an empty house; but why is he there and who is he expecting to meet?

Reading for meaning

1   What is the story of the poem?

2   a)   Why does the poem start with a question?

    b)   What effect does this have on the reader?

3   Which noises from nature contrast with the quietness, between lines 3 and 5, and why are they used?

4   Collect the words describing the listeners.

    a)   How many listeners are there? What sorts of word describe their number?

    b)   Who do you think they are?

5   What do you think of the end of the poem? Is it a good ending? Would you have ended it differently?

The Listeners
Walter de la Mare

'Is there anybody there?' said the Traveller,
　Knocking on the moonlit door;
And his horse in the silence champed the grasses
　Of the forest's ferny floor:
And a bird flew up out of the turret,　　　　　　　　　5
　Above the Traveller's head:
And he smote upon the door again a second time;
　'Is there anybody there?' he said.
But no one descended to the Traveller;
　No head from the leaf-fringed sill　　　　　　　　10
Leaned over and looked into his grey eyes,
　Where he stood perplexed and still.
But only a host of phantom listeners
　That dwelt in the lone house then
Stood listening in the quiet of the moonlight　　　　15
　To that voice from the world of men:
Stood thronging the faint moonbeams on the dark stair,
　That goes down to the empty hall,
Hearkening in an air stirred and shaken
　By the lonely Traveller's call.　　　　　　　　　20
And he felt in his heart their strangeness,
　Their stillness answering his cry,
While his horse moved, cropping the dark turf
　'Neath the starred and leafy sky;
For he suddenly smote on the door, even　　　　　25
　Louder, and lifted his head:—
'Tell them I came, and no one answered,
　That I kept my word,' he said.
Never the least stir made the listeners,
　Though every word he spake　　　　　　　　　30
Fell echoing through the shadowiness of the still house
　From the one man left awake:
Ay, they heard his foot upon the stirrup,
　And the sound of iron on stone,
And how the silence surged softly backward,　　　35
　When the plunging hoofs were gone.

De la Mare's poetic technique

This poem is full of **sounds** that build up to make a very effective piece of writing. Read the poem out loud to discover this. Different poetic techniques are used to add great effect to this narrative poem.

Alliteration is a the term used to describe repetition of sounds, for example: 'forest's ferny floor'. **Onomatopoeia** is the term used to describe words that sound like their meaning, for example: 'bang', 'ping'. **Assonance** is the use of repeated vowel sounds, for example: 'dark' and 'starred'. **Sibilance** is similar to alliteration, but it relates to the repetition of the 's' sound, for example: his horse in the silence champed the grasses.

1 Pick out two examples of **alliteration** and explain why they have been used. *Hint: Look at lines 4 and 35.*

2 Pick out at least five examples of sibilance. What do they contribute to the sense of mystery?

3 De la Mare repeats words as well as sounds. Repetition can be a very good technique if used in moderation. Which words does he repeat? What is the disadvantage of repetition?

Media

Imagine you are going to put a version of 'The Listeners' on film. How would you **storyboard** your ideas to present to a television producer?

Writing to imagine, explore and entertain

There are lots of unanswered questions at the end of this poem. Imagine you are the traveller. Write the story in the **first person** about why you came to the deserted house and what happened afterwards.

● Think about when the story is set, who you are, why you are travelling, and who you want to find in the house.

● Describe how you feel and what sensations you experience. Is it cold? Dark? Can you see here?

● What do you conclude when the door doesn't open?

● What do you do next?

Journey of the Magi

Imagine a story that many of you know quite well. How would it be described if it were told from a different point of view? That is what T. S. Eliot did when he wrote the story of the three kings in his poem.

Before you read

1   Who are the Magi?

2   Create a word web of association for the following key words from the poem: salvation, crucifixion.

Reading for meaning

1   The Magi set out in the dead of winter and experience many problems on their journey. The camels have sore feet and don't want to continue. Look at lines 11–16. What other problems do they have?

2   Why do they decide to travel at night?

3   Look at line 21. Why does everything seem better?

4   The birth of baby Jesus is connected in the poem to his death and how this brings salvation. Look at the image in line 24. What do the three trees remind you of in the crucifixtion story?

5   Why are the Magi no longer at ease after experiencing the events in the poem?

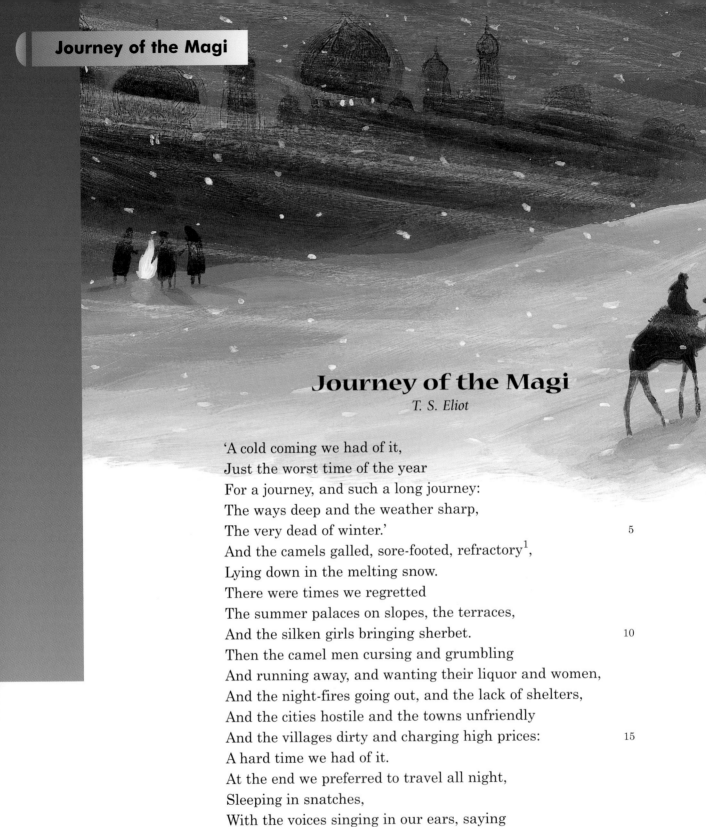

Journey of the Magi

T. S. Eliot

'A cold coming we had of it,
Just the worst time of the year
For a journey, and such a long journey:
The ways deep and the weather sharp,
The very dead of winter.'   5
And the camels galled, sore-footed, refractory[1],
Lying down in the melting snow.
There were times we regretted
The summer palaces on slopes, the terraces,
And the silken girls bringing sherbet.   10
Then the camel men cursing and grumbling
And running away, and wanting their liquor and women,
And the night-fires going out, and the lack of shelters,
And the cities hostile and the towns unfriendly
And the villages dirty and charging high prices: 15
A hard time we had of it.
At the end we preferred to travel all night,
Sleeping in snatches,
With the voices singing in our ears, saying
That this was all folly.   20
Then at dawn we came down to a temperate[2] valley,

1 Irritable
2 Lush

Wet, below the snow line, smelling of vegetation;
With a running stream and a water-mill beating the darkness,
And three trees on the low sky,
And an old white horse galloped away in the meadow.   25
Then we came to a tavern with vine-leaves over the lintel[1],
Six hands at an open door dicing for pieces of silver,
And feet kicking the empty wine-skins[2].
But there was no information, and so we continued
And arrived at evening, not a moment too soon   30
Finding the place; it was (you may say) satisfactory.
All this was a long time ago, I remember,
And I would do it again, but set down
This set down
This: were we led all that way for   35
Birth or Death? There was a Birth, certainly,
We had evidence and no doubt.
I had seen birth and death,
But had thought they were different; this Birth was
Hard and bitter agony for us, like Death, our death.   40
We returned to our places, these kingdoms,
But no longer at ease here, in the old dispensation[3],
With an alien people clutching their gods.
I should be glad of another death.

1 Door frame
2 Wine bottles made of animal hide
3 Old, heathen ways

Language

> **Colloquial language** is a language which sounds as though it is being spoken rather than written. It often includes **slang** or **abbreviations**. For example: It was (you may say) satisfactory.
>
> **Run on lines** are when the line ending of poem does not have a full stop or comma, but goes on to the next line. Eliot uses this poetic technique, for example:
>
> 'Just the worst time of the year
> For a journey, and such a long journey:'

On first reading this poem, you might find the style 'chatty'. There is a lot of repetition of the word 'and' and no obvious **rhyme scheme** or **rhythm**. It is, however, very deliberately written in a colloquial style.

1   Why do you think this is?

2   What is the effect of the run on lines?

Writing to analyse, compare and review

Both 'The Listeners' and 'Journey of the Magi' poems have very distinct and unexpected endings. Give your opinion of both of them.

1   Write an analysis of the effects the two poets are trying to achieve.

2   Which poem do you prefer and why?

Use quotations from the poems to support your answers.

Writing to describe a viewpoint

Choose a common, well-known story. It could be a myth, legend, Bible story or from another holy book. For example: Mohammed's journey from Mecca to Medina; Robin Hood; Little Red Riding Hood. Now try to look at the story from a slightly different viewpoint. Tell the story from a different angle, just as T. S. Eliot has in his poem.

Review

What did you particularly enjoy in this chapter?

What did you not like very much?

Was there anything:

- you found difficult to understand?

- you discovered or understood for the first time?

Use this checklist to help you answer these questions and review the progress you have made.

- **You have read**: two modern poems, one extract from a children's novel, one diary extract, two autobiographies and one piece of travel writing.

- **You have thought about how writers use**: techniques such as rhyme, assonance, alliteration, sibilance, onomatopoeia and personification; different genres of writing such as travel writing, diaries and autobiography and first and third person narrative.

- **To improve your writing, you have thought about**: spelling – archaic and modern words, prefixes and suffixes; sentence level skills – composition and effect of clauses, adjectives and adverbs, sentence length and context; planning and text level skills; spider diagrams, flow charts, underlining and highlighting, story boards, writing frames.

- **You have written to**: imagine, explore and entertain – a prediction narrative; inform, persuade and argue – a diary, letter and a newspaper article; compare, persuade and argue – a discursive essay; analyse, compare and review – a comparative essay; expressing a viewpoint – narrative from a different person.

- **Your speaking and listening has included**: a role play and performance; discussing texts in pairs, groups and as a class.

- **You may have used ICT to**: use the Internet for research; to tabulate your answers; to create a storyboard; spellcheck and present final drafts of your writing neatly and attractively.

Myths and legends

Storytelling has been a favourite pastime since the dawn of time. The stories told have been touched with superstition, fear of the unknown and the imaginations of those who have told them. The result? A rich and amazing variety of tales. The following chapter contains but a few.

2.1 Legendary creatures

In this section you will encounter some monstrous and mysterious creatures which have terrified and fascinated people for hundreds of years. Many of these creatures have captured the imagination to such an extent that people will travel into dangerous situations to find out the truth.

King of the Cloud Forests

The following text is from 'King of the Cloud Forests' by Michael Morpurgo.

Before you read

In pairs, talk about any monstrous and mysterious creatures you know of.

a) What type of creature are they?

b) What legends or stories are told about them?

c) Why do they arouse such interest?

> I watched Uncle Sung stumble away through the deep drifts, leaning heavily on his staff. The last I saw of him he was turning and waving back at me, knee deep in snow, and then I was alone with only his footprints outside to remind me I was not the only person alive in this white wilderness.
>
> I set about the task he had left me with a will and banked up the fire with all the fuel that was left in the hut – and that was not much. I boiled some water and sat by the fire, filling myself with warmth. In spite of this my legs below the knees remained numb. My legs and feet were there because I could see them but I had long since

ceased to feel them. I went to the window and scanned the snow around the hut again for any sign of the wolves. There wasn't a footprint or scat anywhere – it was all virgin white and unblemished except for Uncle Sung's tracks. I decided it was safe to go out. I was too weak to hurry. I trudged back and forth to the sheds until the back of our hut was piled high with dung and food.

Reading for meaning

1   This story is told in the **first person narrative**. Who is the narrator? What state of mind is he in? Why?

2   What can you tell about his relationship with his Uncle Sung? What job had his Uncle Sung left him with? Why had he left him this job?

3   Find three different words or phrases which describe his environment.

First person narrative is a technique used by a writer when the story is told through the eyes of a character involved in the story. You can recognise first person narrative by the use of **I**, **my** and **me** in the text. For example: **I** was on **my** way back.
Third person narrative is the technique used when someone from outside the story is narrating events. For example: **He** walked back to the hut.

It was early afternoon by now and I was on my way back with an armful of lightings just in case the fire ever went out and we had to start it again. I was thinking how pleased Uncle Sung would be with me when he saw what I had done, and then I saw the prints, a second track running almost parallel with Uncle Sung's. He was back, back already. In my eagerness I stumbled in the snow and dropped the sticks around me. I never bothered to pick them up. They could wait. There would be food inside. I threw open the door.

Reading for meaning

1 What do you notice about the way Michael Morpurgo writes this paragraph? *Hint: Look at the types of sentence he uses and how this changes.*

2 What is the difference in mood when the narrator sees the extra set of footsteps? What causes the change in mood?

3 There is a creature waiting inside the hut. What kind of creature do you think it is?

4 a) Take the paragraph which starts 'It was early afternoon…' and change the narrative viewpoint from first person to third person.

   b) In what ways does this change the paragraph?

The creature was crouched by the fire and when he rose his bulk filled the room. He was like a giant man but yet not a man, for he was covered in a coat of long, red hair.

I could neither run nor scream. Even when the huge creature lumbered towards me I remained rooted to the spot. Because my head was swimming I raised my hand to steady myself against the door. As I did so the creature stopped instantly, mouth open, breathing hard. He was close to me now, towering above me. Only then did my thoughts gather themselves and it came to me that this might be the yeti creature Uncle Sung had described to me. He was gigantic and was covered in red hair from head to toe. Only the centre of the face was hairless. The skin was wrinkled and black. His nose was flat and turned up so that the nostrils were scarcely more than two holes in his face, and the chin receded almost formless into his neck. His forehead was vast and prominent and overhung the face in a permanent frown. But under the thick red eyebrows the eyes that looked down at me were searching and intelligent. They were wide with fear or anger – I could not tell which.

Keeping an arm's length away he circled around towards the open door. He stood for a moment examining me, his head slightly on one side before turning and ducking under the door. It took me some time to come to my senses. I slammed the door shut after him and ran to the window. The yeti, and I was now quite sure that that was what he was, was bounding away through the snow on all fours. Beyond the barn he stopped, and turned and stood up again. For just a moment he looked at me, and then he was gone and I was alone again. Curiously enough after such a terrifying encounter I can remember that I was sad to see him go. There was no sense of relief that danger had passed, just a feeling that I had somehow wasted an opportunity. Worst of all was the knowledge that I was alone again in this desolate place with only my hunger for company. I felt oppressed by the new emptiness around me.

How much I longed now for Uncle Sung to return and for the food I knew he would bring with him. But as time passed I began to believe that Uncle Sung might not ever come back and that I would be left to die here on my own. The wind got up again whipping the world outside into a raging blizzard. The hut shook so violently that I thought the roof would lift off at any moment. I knew that Uncle Sung could not travel in such weather. No man could.

I piled the fire high again and drank more hot water, not because I was thirsty, more to banish the desperate loneliness and fear that welled inside me. Certainly the crackle and the heat of the fire was some comfort. But sleep was the only real way to forget and I slept in snatches all through that day and into the night. I spent my waking hours keeping a futile watch at the window for any sign of Uncle Sung's return. The end of the blizzard brought a welcome silence but no hope. There was no movement outside. The fresh snow had covered all footprints and tracks. It was as if neither Uncle Sung nor the yeti had ever been here.

Once in the half light of dawn I fancied I saw a shadowy figure stalking through the snow in the distance. It might have been a wolf, a bear or perhaps a yeti. Whatever it was I welcomed it, for it was some sign that I was not the only thing left alive in this white wasteland. I was quite beyond being frightened of anything by now.

The next day was the longest I ever knew. I busied myself trying to drive some feeling into my ankles and feet, stamping up and down the hut, but that tired me quickly, and my feet stayed frozen despite all my efforts. To pass the time I began to build a lifesize effigy of my yeti in the ash that was piled in front of the fire. I tried it again and again until I felt it was a fair representation of the creature I had seen. By the time I had finished the ash yeti was stretched out like a giant gingerbread man right across the room in front of the fire. I found two black stones for his eyes, a stick for his mouth, and it was done. And still Uncle Sung did not come. I waited by the window all afternoon and watched the sun slip behind the mountain peaks and the shadow of night creep across the snow towards me. He did not come and he did not come. He would never come.

That night I curled up in front of the fire and tried to rock myself to sleep. I was sure by now that Uncle Sung had either been taken by the wolves or that he had lost his way in the mountains or had been caught out in the blizzard and had perished with the cold. I knew for certain that Uncle Sung was dead and when I cried it was for him and for me because I knew there could be no hope now for either of us. It was the end.

I slipped in and out of turbulent and terrifying nightmares and was no longer conscious of the passing time or of cold or of hunger. Lin, Uncle Sung, the lama and a pack of ravenous golden wolves peopled these nightmares and recurrent in all of them was the yeti – 'Red' I called him – who saved us all time and time again. I had been fending off the wolves with my staff and I was about to be torn apart when Red came bounding across the snow and drove them off. I was not at all surprised at this for he had done it often enough before – he always seemed to arrive just in time. He was bending over me asking if I was hurt when I noticed he was not alone. There were two of them peering into my face. Then they began to sniff and lick me from head to toe, and I didn't care much for that. The feel of their hot breath on my ear tickled me and I pushed them away and sat up, dreading as I did so the abandonment of my dreams and the return to the reality of my living nightmare. But it was no dream.

The two yetis sat back on their haunches in front of me and studied me closely. The first I recognised at once as the yeti I had come to know as Red in my dreams, but the second was clearly older. He was white about the head and beard. The skin of his face was darker, more heavily creased and more deeply etched with wrinkles. He seemed only to have one ear, though it was difficult to tell through the hair. His eyes glinted gold in the fire. They were talking to each other, or perhaps it was to me, for they never took their eyes off me. It was hardly a language as we know it, more a sequence of curious moans and whimpers, but nonetheless formed and deliberately intoned. It was not the insane hysterical chattering

of a monkey that I was listening to, but considered speech, however unintelligible it might have been to me.

I looked from one to the other. The older yeti – for that is what I presumed the white hair indicated – reached out slowly and touched me on the hair. I had not realised until then how extraordinarily long their arms were. The hand was leathery on the inside and black, and the thumb was as long as the other fingers. I shrank back but the arm seemed to stretch out after me like elastic. The touch on my face was smooth and leathery. His eyes looked into mine and there was a gentleness that calmed me at once. He arranged his lips carefully, and then she spoke, "Leelee," he said, first to me and then to Red. "Leelee," and then both of them together. "Leelee," their voices high with excitement. "Leelee! Leelee! Leelee!" It seemed a sound I could imitate, and so I talked back to them and ventured a smile. "Leelee," I said, surprised at the strength in my own voice. Smiles wreathed their faces, revealing jagged, discoloured teeth. It was then that Red noticed my ash effigy. For some moments they considered it together and then broke into peals of screeching laughter, piling more and more ash on the stomach to make it fatter. Before I knew it Red had lifted me off my feet and was hugging me so tight that I had to struggle for breath. To fight against such strength would not have been possible anyway, but there seemed little reason to struggle against them because these were hugs of affection. They passed me from one to the other like a precious doll. It was as if they had to hug me to believe I was real. Satisfied at last that I was, they squatted down before the fire to warm themselves, looking across at me from time to time and uttering whimpers of delight. It was a few moments later before I realised they were not just warming themselves. There was a sudden sweet smell of roasting meat. Crouched over the fire the two yetis turned and prodded the hunk of meat that lay buried in the bed of red ashes. By the smell I supposed it to be mutton, but I did not care what it was. It seemed an eternity before they rolled it out onto the floor, wrenched it apart

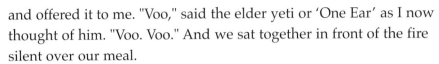

and offered it to me. "Voo," said the elder yeti or 'One Ear' as I now thought of him. "Voo. Voo." And we sat together in front of the fire silent over our meal.

I devoured mine like a mad creature, licking my fingers until the last taste of meat was gone. No matter that it was burned on the outside and raw on the inside, no matter that I ate so fast I nearly choked. My gorging was watched with delight by the two yetis who imitated me licking my fingers. "Leelee," they cried. "Leelee!" And they set to hugging me all over again. So I thought little of it when some time later One Ear picked me up again. I braced myself as he hugged me, but then he dumped me on Red's back, and before I knew it I was outside the door, a rush of cold wind on my face and One Ear was bounding ahead on all fours through the snow.

As Red followed, I clung on round his neck and gripped his sides with my knees. Twice in those first few yards I came off and tumbled into the snow. He laughed and waited for me to clamber on again before setting off after One Ear, springing almost immediately into a run. I curled my fingers into his hair, laid myself along the back of his neck and hung on like a leech. I had had a horse bolt under me once before and this was a similar experience, but after the first few minutes it was not so alarming as I felt Red wanted me to stay on. As my confidence grew I relaxed, and the flow and the rhythm of his legs under me became easier to anticipate and to ride. Until then I had been so busy trying not to fall off that I had not even thought about where they were taking me or why, and even now I was not that concerned about it. I only knew that they had found me and fed me, that they had greeted me like some long lost friend. I was elated perhaps by the speed at which we travelled, faster than any horse I had ever ridden, but more I think because I knew that my ordeal by hunger was at last over.

Every few minutes they would stop and I noticed they always slowed down together and came to a halt precisely at the same moment, seemingly without any signal or word passing between them. One Ear would rear up onto his back legs and lift his nose into the wind, while beneath me I could feel Red's body taut with concentration. For a few moments they would listen and watch, still as statues; and then the rocking journey would begin again. We climbed all that day, speeding effortlessly through the snow. The valley bottoms were hidden now under the clouds, and by that evening we had only the blue of the sky above us. We were, it seemed, travelling on the top of the world, and the yetis kept up this relentless pace, stopping less frequently now. My hands and fingers were so numb by this time that only the failing strength of my arms kept me from sliding off. My legs were quite useless below the knees. I had nothing to grip with. Red seemed to sense this for from time to time he would stop and a great arm would reach out from under me and arrange me so that my balance was restored.

As dark came on we had left the peaks above us and were making a slow and difficult descent across rock-strewn glaciers. Crevasses and chasms that looked impassable we leapt with consummate ease. Then we were in amongst sparse pine trees that clung impossibly to the mountainside and as the last of the light vanished we were swallowed quite suddenly by a dense forest that shut out the last of the day.

We stopped and I let myself down gently for I could not feel my feet as they touched the ground. There was a hurried hushed conversation between One Ear and Red and then to my astonishment I saw One Ear climb high into the tree beside us and swing away through the canopy of the trees until I could see him no more. I thought for one terrible moment as Red picked me up that we would follow him, but instead, with Red clasping me to his chest with one arm and my legs wrapped around him, we moved slowly through the undergrowth. It was the most painful part of the journey. Twigs and branches tore at me so that to protect myself I buried my face in Red's chest and closed my eyes.

59

It was some hours later when at last he stopped and set me down on my feet. I could see we were in a small clearing. There was the smell of wood smoke in the air and excited whispers from somewhere ahead of us in the darkness. Red led me along a path beside a black cliff face and then I saw a flickering glow emerging from the cliff some distance away. "Leelee!" Red called out beside me. "Leelee!" And then One Ear was there in front of us, his face lit up. He held out his hand, and so with Red on one side and One Ear on the other I was led in through the mouth of the cave. The strong light dazzled me at first. I could make out many figures, perhaps a dozen or more running towards us. A great fire in the centre revealed a vast cavern which seemed to stretch back into the cliff as far as the eye could see. I felt myself hoisted suddenly up onto Red's shoulders as the crowd of yetis rushed towards us. "Leelee!" they chanted. "Leelee!" And every one of them it seemed wanted to touch some part of me. My hands and knees were squeezed and patted, my fingers prised apart examined and smelt. I could see that many of them had tears in their eyes.

Each one of them was different. There were a few with tawny, rust coloured hair, but none were the colour of 'Red'. Many had a greyer coat. It was clear at once that there were several old ones amongst them for they were white around the face like One Ear – and it was in particular these older yetis that seemed overcome, almost ecstatic at my arrival. I felt famous. I felt adored. The young yetis, some of them even smaller than me, were plucked from their mothers and held up to touch me, but most of these were terrified and screamed to be put down, much it seemed to everyone else's amusement.

Then I noticed one young yeti who had fallen in beside us and was walking with us now, his hand in Red's. He was looking up at me, but his was no adoring look. Instead there was a cold glare in his eyes that forced me to turn away. He was almost the same colour as Red and I thought of them at once as father and son. They were too alike to be otherwise. One Ear stood on a rock in the centre of the cave, his back to the fire, and made a speech, not a word of which I could understand of course, save the word that I took by now to be the name by which they knew me, "Leelee". He kept pointing to a crudely fashioned, four-legged stool beside him on the rock. A chorus of raucous shrieking heralded a ceremony that I can only describe as a kind of coronation.

Almost solemnly One Ear took my hand and helped me up onto the rock. He led me towards the stool. It was clear I was expected to sit. As I did so a thunderous cheer went up. I thought then of the lama's 'mo', that I should one day soon be a king, 'king of the cloud forest', and I wished that Uncle Sung could be with me to witness it.

The seat of the stool beneath me was solid enough but I felt the legs were loose. It wobbled precariously. I could see no other piece of furniture in the cave and was wondering how it came to be there when Red approached me holding in his hands a small painted tin. There were faces on the outside of it, faces I thought I recognised but could not identify. A sudden silence fell on the cave. They were waiting for me to do something. I could think of nothing else but to reach down and take the box that he seemed to be offering to me. I put it down on my knees. There was writing on it. 'E.A.' in large letters, and then 'Coronation of King Edward VII and Queen Alexandra. One Shilling'. I opened it. It was almost empty, except for an old photograph, a knife with a bone handle and a briar pipe.

"Leelee!" They cried. "Leelee! Leelee!" I smiled at them and held up the tin. This appeared was the proper response for the cheering broke out again. Looking around me I saw only one of them was not ecstatically happy. 'Little Red', as I called him, stood by his father and looked straight into my eyes. It was a look of naked hatred.

Reading for meaning

1 How does Michael feel after the yeti leaves the hut? What impact does this feeling, plus the physical conditions he is experiencing, have on his state of mind? Use words and phrases from the text to illustrate your answer.

2 What is Michael's first reaction to the yetis?

3 What do we learn about the yeti way of life from this chapter?

4 In what ways are the yetis similar to humans? In what ways are they dissimilar to humans?

5 What do you find most surprising about the yeti lifestyle described by Michael Morpurgo?

6 At the end of the chapter, Little Red looked into Michael's eyes with 'a look of naked hatred'. What reason does he have for disliking Michael?

Vocabulary and spelling

1 Re-read the paragraph beginning 'I could neither run nor scream' on page 54. Write out phrases used to describe the yeti. You should be looking for phrases which describe the yeti's size, appearance, colour and movement.

2 Underline the adjectives in the same paragraph. What impression of this creature do the adjectives create?

3 What spelling rules about word endings are illustrated by the following words from the passage: 'raging', 'piling', 'whipping', 'running'?

4 For each of the words listed below, find another appropriate adjective to replace it. You should use a thesaurus to help you: 'prominent', 'turbulent', 'recurrent', 'consummate', 'ecstatic'.

5 A writer creates atmosphere through the choice of vivid vocabulary. Find these phrases and explain why the author has used them: 'thunderous cheer', 'raucous shrieking', 'they chanted'.

Sentences, paragraphs and punctuation

Look at the paragraph on page 55 beginning 'The next day was the longest I ever knew'.

1   In the opening sentence the writer uses the past tense **I knew** instead of the past perfect tense **I had known**. Why do you think the author has chosen to use the past tense?

2   The next sentence is long. Rewrite it in four separate sentences. What is the effect of writing it in four sentences? Explain which version is better and why.

3   In contrast, the last two sentences are short and the writer uses repetition. What does the use of repetition tell us about the narrator?

Reading for meaning

1 Where would you find the piece of writing on page 65?

2 What clues are there in the writing style?

3 Is this piece of writing fact or fiction? How can you tell?

Research

Using the Internet, search for information on the yeti or the 'abominable snowman'. You should use a **search engine** to help you locate this information. Read the information and record all of the details about the yeti in **note** form.

Writing to inform, explain and describe

You are now going to use this information to create an entry for the *Rough Guide to the Himalaya*s, under the heading 'Yeti – the Abominable Snowman'.

You will need to give background information about the yeti (legends, superstitions), scientific comment and advice about how to deal with a potential encounter.

You will also need to think about:

• layout and presentation – keep it easy to read and attractive.

• style of writing – you need to inform your reader, but you may also want to entertain and give advice!

Beijing, China

January 13, 1998: Associated Press Release

The Yeti, or Abominable Snowman, is nothing
more than an ordinary brown bear, according to
a Chinese wildlife expert who has been
following the traces of the mysterious creature
for more than 10 years. Liu Wulin, head of the
Wildlife Protection Office in Tibet, said fur
and pawprints left behind by the beast belong
to a bear. "It must be bears leaving those
marks that lack an arch, but the pads really
resemble man's", he was quoted by the official
Xinhua news agency Tuesday as saying. He
blamed Tibetan legends for turning the bear
into a monster with long, red hair. "Even if
the yeti did exist it would be doomed to
extinction because of its tiny population and
inbreeding."

> The Sirens were beautiful creatures, half-woman, half-bird, who sang such sweet songs that listeners forgot everything and died of hunger. The Sirens were sisters who lured sailors to their death. The song of the Sirens was irresistible.
>
> There were many Sirens, including:
>
> - Parthenope (maiden face)
> - Ligea (shrill)
> - Leucosia (white being)
> - Aglaope (beautiful face)
> - Aglaophonos (beautiful voice)
> - Molpe (music)
> - Teles (perfect)
> - Raidne (improvement)

Vocabulary: learn some Greek

1   Look at the names of the two Sirens called Aglaope and Aglaophonos. Which part of the word means beautiful? What do the remaining parts of the words – 'pe' and 'phonos' – mean?

2   Using 'phonos' as the stem, write five words that belong to the same family. What do these words mean? For example: micro<u>phone</u> – a device used to increase the volume of sound.

The Odyssey

The Sirens appear in an epic story called 'The Odyssey', written by Homer, a Greek poet. 'The Odyssey' tells the tale of Odysseus and the adventures he encounters on his voyage home after the Trojan Wars.

The extract concerns his encounter with the Sirens. Odysseus has been talking to Circe, a goddess, who wants to help him to find his way home. She gives him some advice about what he should do…

The Odyssey

'As Circe came to an end, Dawn took her golden throne. The gracious goddess left me and made her way inland, while I went to my ship and ordered my men to embark and loose the hawsers. They did so promptly, went to the benches, sat down in their places and struck the grey surf with their oars. Then the fair Circe, that formidable goddess with a woman's voice, sent us the friendly escort of a favourable wind, which sprang up from astern and filled the sail of our blue-painted ship. We set the tackle in order fore and aft and then sat down, while the wind and the helmsman kept her on course.

'I was much perturbed in spirit and before long took my men into my confidence. "My friends," I said, "it is not right that only one or two of us should know the prophecies that Circe, in her divine wisdom, has made to me, and I am going to pass them on to you, so that you may all be forewarned, whether we die or escape the worst and save our lives. Her first warning concerned the mysterious Sirens. We must beware of their song and give their flowery meadow a wide berth. I alone, she suggested, might listen to their voices; but you must bind me hard and fast, so that I cannot stir from the spot where you will stand me, by the step of the mast, with the rope's ends lashed round the mast itself. And if I beg you to release me, you must tighten and add to my bonds."

'I thus explained every detail to my men. In the meantime our good ship, with that perfect wind to drive her, fast approached the Sirens' Isle. But now the breeze dropped, some power lulled the waves, and a breathless calm set in. Rising from their seats my men drew in the sail and threw it into the hold, then sat down at the oars and churned the water white with their blades of polished pine. Meanwhile I took a large round of wax, cut it up small with my sword, and kneaded the pieces with all the strength of my fingers. The wax soon yielded to my vigorous treatment and grew warm, for I had the rays of my Lord, the Sun to help me.

'I took each of my men in turn and plugged their ears with it. They then made me a prisoner on my ship by binding me hand and foot, standing me up by the step of the mast and tying the rope's ends to the mast itself. This done, they sat down once more and struck grey water with their oars.

'We made good progress and had just come within a call of the shore when the Sirens became aware that a ship was swiftly bearing down upon them, and they broke into their liquid song.

' "Draw near," they sang, "illustrious Odysseus, flower of Achaean chivalry, and bring your ship to rest so that you may hear our voices. No seaman ever sailed his black ship past this spot without listening to the sweet tones that flow from our lips, and none that listened has not been delighted and gone on a wiser man. For we know all that the Argives and Trojans suffered on the broad plain of Troy by the will of the gods, and we have foreknowledge of all that is going to happen in this fruitful earth."

'The lovely voices came to me across the water, and my heart was filled with such a longing to listen that with nod and frown I signed my men to set me free. But they swung forward their oars and rowed ahead, while Perimedes and Eurylochus jumped up, tightened my bonds and added more. However, when they had rowed past the Sirens and we could no longer hear their voices and the burden of their song, my good companions were quick to clear their ears of the wax I had used to stop them, and to free me from my shackles.'

Reading for meaning

1 What do you find out about the relationship between:

a) Odysseus and Circe

b) Odysseus and his men?

Use quotation from the text to support your answer.

2 What special powers does the goddess, Circe, possess?

3 Circe is described as 'that formidable goddess with a woman's voice'. Why do you think this expression is used?

4 Why is the Sirens' song first of all described as 'liquid' and then a 'burden'?

5 What device is being used in this phrase taken from the first line of the extract, 'Dawn took her golden throne'?

6 Find an additional example of this device from the extract.

7 What language techniques are used by the Sirens to persuade Odysseus to stop and listen to their song?

Vocabulary

1 Note down all the words and phrases used to describe **nautical** activity in the extract.

2 From your own knowledge, add at least three words or phrases which are nautical terms and explain their meaning.

Sentences

'They did so promptly, went to their benches, sat down in their places and struck the grey surf with their oars.'

1 a) What do you notice about the organisation of this sentence?

b) What effect is created by choosing to construct the sentence in this way?

2 Find three examples of the same type of sentence construction from the extract.

3 Make up your own sentence, based on this construction style, to describe how the sirens sang their song.

Speaking and listening

'… we know all that the Argives and Trojans suffered on the broad plain of Troy…'

Here the Sirens refer to the fact that Odysseus had been fighting in the Trojan Wars.

1   Find out all you can about the Trojan Wars. Use these questions to help you.

- Who was fighting?

- Why were they fighting?

- Where did the wars take place?

- What famous event happened?

 2   Once you have gathered your information, prepare then role-play an interview with Odysseus, asking questions about his experiences in the Trojan Wars.

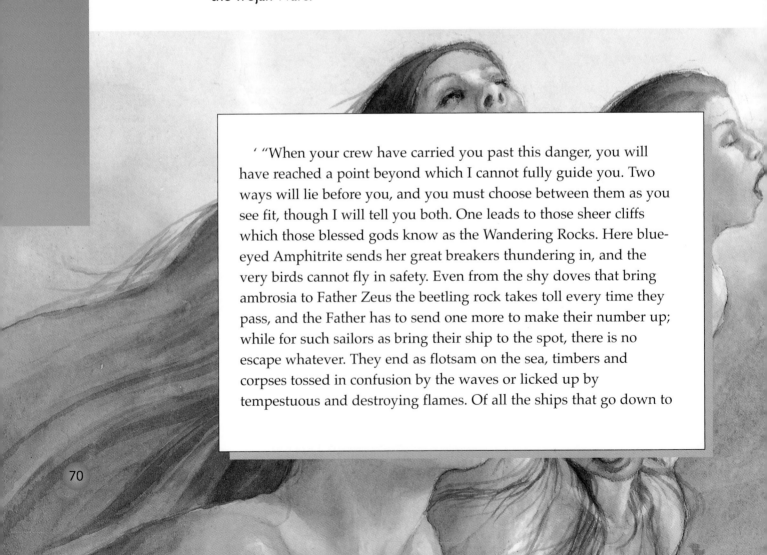

' "When your crew have carried you past this danger, you will have reached a point beyond which I cannot fully guide you. Two ways will lie before you, and you must choose between them as you see fit, though I will tell you both. One leads to those sheer cliffs which those blessed gods know as the Wandering Rocks. Here blue-eyed Amphitrite sends her great breakers thundering in, and the very birds cannot fly in safety. Even from the shy doves that bring ambrosia to Father Zeus the beetling rock takes toll every time they pass, and the Father has to send one more to make their number up; while for such sailors as bring their ship to the spot, there is no escape whatever. They end as flotsam on the sea, timbers and corpses tossed in confusion by the waves or licked up by tempestuous and destroying flames. Of all the ships that go down to the sea one only has made the passage, and that was the celebrated Argo, homeward bound from Aeetes' coast. And she would soon have been dashed upon those mighty crags, if Hera, for love of Jason, had not helped her past.

' "In the other direction lie two rocks, the higher of which rears its peak up to the very sky and is capped by black clouds that never stream away nor leave clear weather round the top, even in summer or at harvest-time. No man on earth could climb it, up or down, not even with twenty hands and feet to help him; for the rock is smooth as if it had been polished. But half-way up the crag is a misty cavern, facing the West and running down to Erebus, past which, my lord Odysseus, you must steer your ship. The strongest bowman could not reach the gaping mouth of the cave with an arrow shot from a ship below. It is the home of Scylla, the creature with the dreadful bark. It is true that her bark is no louder than a new-born pup's, but she is a horrible monster nevertheless, and one whom nobody could look at with delight, not even a god if he passed that way. She has twelve feet, all dangling in the air, and six long necks, each ending in a grisly head with triple rows of teeth, set thick and close, and darkly menacing death. Up to her middle she is sunk in the depths of the cave, but her heads protrude from the fearful abyss, and thus she fishes from her own abode, scouting around the rock for any dolphin or swordfish she may catch, or any of the larger monsters which in their thousands find their living in the roaring seas. No crew can boast that they ever sailed their ship past Scylla without loss, since from every passing vessel she snatches a man with each of her heads and so bears off her prey.

' "The other of the two rocks is lower, as you, Odysseus, will see, and the distance between them is no more than a bowshot. A great fig-tree with luxuriant foliage grows upon the crag, and it is below this that dread Charybdis sucks the dark waters down. Three times a day she spews them up, and three times she swallows them down once more in her horrible way. Heaven keep you from the spot when she is at her work, for not even the Earthshaker could save you from disaster. No: you must hug Scylla's rock and with all speed drive your ship through, since it is far better that you should have to

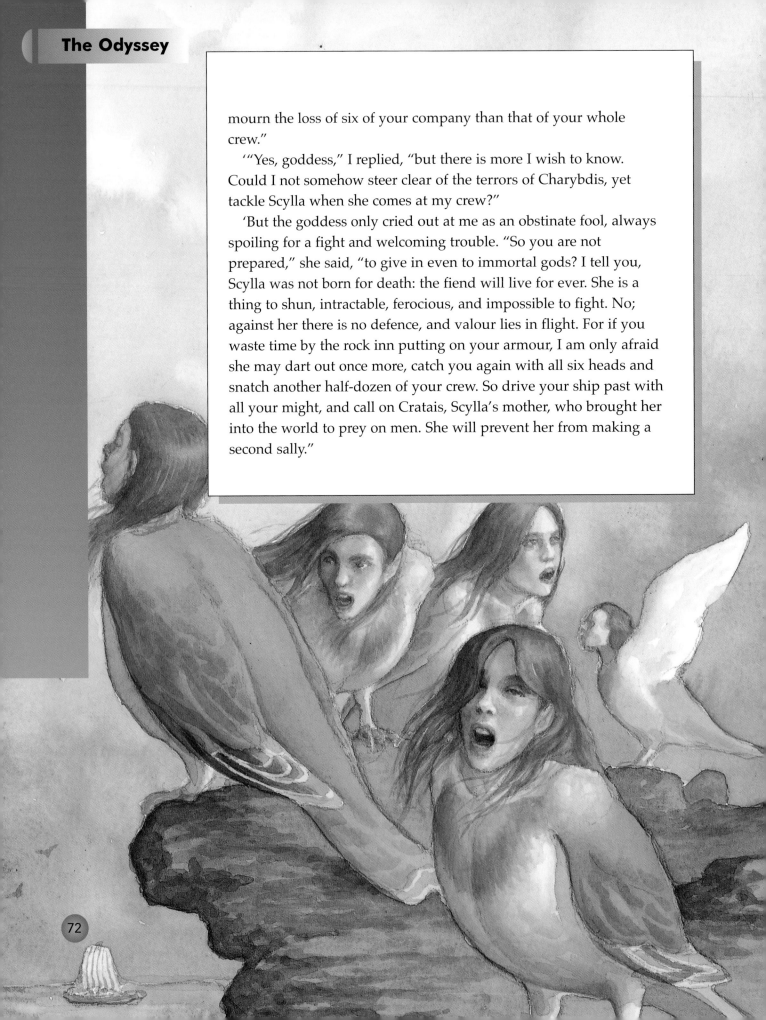

mourn the loss of six of your company than that of your whole crew."

'"Yes, goddess," I replied, "but there is more I wish to know. Could I not somehow steer clear of the terrors of Charybdis, yet tackle Scylla when she comes at my crew?"

'But the goddess only cried out at me as an obstinate fool, always spoiling for a fight and welcoming trouble. "So you are not prepared," she said, "to give in even to immortal gods? I tell you, Scylla was not born for death: the fiend will live for ever. She is a thing to shun, intractable, ferocious, and impossible to fight. No; against her there is no defence, and valour lies in flight. For if you waste time by the rock inn putting on your armour, I am only afraid she may dart out once more, catch you again with all six heads and snatch another half-dozen of your crew. So drive your ship past with all your might, and call on Cratais, Scylla's mother, who brought her into the world to prey on men. She will prevent her from making a second sally."

Reading for meaning

List all of the things you learn about the appearance and behaviour of:

a) Scylla

b) Charybdis

Vocabulary

Scylla and Charybdis are both monsters. They could be described as 'bad', but this would not give us a sufficiently clear picture.

1 Explore the evidence about how 'bad' Scylla and Charybdis actually are. Write down ten adjectives to describe them, listing the adjectives from bad to worst.

2 Now, think about their appearance and movements. List ten adjectives and ten verbs to describe what they look like and how they move.

3 Using this word bank, write a paragraph describing:

    a) Scylla

    b) Charybdis

    Use vivid and specific vocabulary to create a word picture of these two creatures.

Writing to inform, explain and describe

Using the information given by Circe in the extract, write step-by-step instructions for Odysseus. Make sure you clearly identify what Odysseus must do to ensure he, his ship and his men negotiate this terrible and dangerous place safely.

Siren Song

by Margaret Atwood

This is the one song everyone
would like to learn: the song
that is irresistible:

the song that forces men
to leap overboard in squadrons   5
even though they see the bleached skulls

the song nobody knows
because anyone who has heard it
is dead, and the others can't remember.

shall I tell you the secret   10
and if I do, will you get me
out of this bird suit?

I don't enjoy it here
squatting on this island
looking picturesque and mythical   15

with these two feathery maniacs,
I don't enjoy singing
this trio, fatal and valuable.

I will tell the secret to you,
to you, only to you.   20
Come closer. This song

is a cry for help: Help me!
Only you, only you can,
you are unique

at last. Alas
it is a boring song   25
but it works every time.

Siren Song

Reading for meaning

1 In your own words, describe the feelings of the narrator at the beginning of this poem. What words and phrases tell you this?

2 What is the effect of the question in stanza 4?

3 a) How does the listener feel about the siren?

   b) By the end of the poem, how have your sympathies changed? Why?

4 a) What tense is used in the poem?

   b) Why do you think Margaret Atwood uses this particular tense?

5 What do you notice about the use of **personal pronouns**?

> *I, you, he, she, we* and *they* are all **personal pronouns**.

6 a) What do you notice about the length of the lines?

   b) What choices has the poet made about where to start a new line?

7 The poem is arranged in short stanzas. Comment on the way the poem is laid out and why you think Margaret Atwood has organised the poem in this way.

8 Why are sirens women? Would the story work as well if they were men?

Margaret Atwood's poetic technique

1 What effect is achieved by the repetition in stanza 8?

2 Look closely at the first line of the last stanza. This is an example of **assonance**.
   What effect is created by the repetition of the vowel sound?

Vocabulary and spelling

1   Look up the meaning of 'squadrons' in line 5. Why do you think Margaret Atwood has chosen to use this word?

2   What does the word 'squatting' suggest about the narrator?

3   In pairs, look closely at the following words and phrases from the poem. Write them down and **annotate** them with your ideas and questions; feathery maniacs; fatal and valuable; bleached skulls; looking picturesque and mythical; will you get me out of this bird suit?; I will tell the secret to you to you, only to you.

> To **annotate** something means to make notes about it. When we annotate a word or phrase, we write notes around them.

Writing to imagine, explore and entertain

How do you think a listener would respond to the sirens' song? Write four sentences which describe how the man listening to Margaret Atwood's sirens might respond. Use the following questions to help you imagine his feelings:

- What was the man doing as he became aware of the siren song?

- What was the first thing he heard?

- What interested him about the words of the song?

- What did the song sound like?

- How does he feel about the siren singing this song?

Use the answers to help you write a paragraph that describes the listener's encounter with the sirens. Once you have written your paragraph, reorganise your sentences using the same style as Margaret Atwood and create the first four stanzas (or more) of a poem entitled 'The Listener's Voice'.

2.3 Old wives' tales

Mrs Number Three

In her introduction to the book of fairy tales, from which this story is taken, Angela Carter, the author, says, 'This is a collection of old wives' tales, put together with the intention of giving pleasure, and with a good deal of pleasure on my part. These stories have only one thing in common — they all centre around a female protagonist; be she clever, or brave, or good, or silly, or cruel, or sinister, or awesomely unfortunate, she is at centre stage, as large as life…'

Before you read

1 In pairs, discuss any fairy tales that you know well which contain a central female character.

● What type of character is she?

● What part does she play in the story?

Look at Angela Carter's definitions of the female protagonist to start you off in your discussions. Record your information on a table to help organise your ideas.

2 a) Share your ideas with the rest of the class. Briefly describe the plot, who the main female character is and what type of character she is.

b) Listen carefully to the contributions and add further detail to your table.

Mrs Number Three

During the T'ang Period there stood, to the west of the city of K'ai Feng Fu, an inn called the 'Footbridge Tavern', kept by a woman about thirty years of age. No one knew who she was or whence she came, and she was known locally as 'Mrs Number Three'. She was childless, had no relations, and was supposed to be a widow. It was a comfortable, roomy inn; the hostess was in easy circumstances, and had a herd of very fine asses.

Besides this, she had a generous nature. If a traveller were short of money, she would reduce her prices, or board him for nothing; so her inn was never empty.

Some time between AD 806 and 820, a man called Chao Chi Ho, on his way to Lo Yang (which was then the capital city of China), stopped at the 'Footbridge Tavern' for the night. There were six or seven guests there already, each of whom had a bed in a large sleeping apartment. Chao, the last arrival, had a bed allotted to him in a corner, against the wall of the hostess's bedroom. Mrs Number Three treated him well, as she did all her guests. At bedtime she offered wine to each, and took a glass with them. Chao alone had none, as he did not generally drink wine. Quite late, when all the guests had gone to bed, the hostess retired to her room, shut the door and blew out the light.

The other guests were soon snoring peacefully, but Chao felt restless.

About midnight he heard the hostess moving things about in her room, and peeped through a crack in the wall. She lit a candle, and took out of a box an ox, a drover and a plough, little wooden models about six or seven inches high. She placed them near the hearth, on the beaten-clay floor of the room, took some water in her mouth, and sprayed it over the figures. Immediately they came to life. The drover goaded the ox, which drew the plough, back and forth, furrowing the

floor over a space about equal to that of an ordinary mat. When the ploughing was done, she handed the drover a packet of buckwheat grains. He sowed them, and they at once began to sprout. In a few minutes they flowered, and then bore ripe grain. The drover gathered the grain, threshed it, and handed it to Mrs Number Three, who made him grind it in a little mill. Then she put the drover, his ox and his plough – which had again become little wooden figures – back into their box and used the buckwheat flour to make cakes.

At cockcrow the guests arose and prepared to leave, but the hostess said, 'You must not go without breakfast,' and set the buckwheat cakes before them.

Chao was very uneasy, so he thanked her and walked out of the inn. Looking over his shoulder, he saw each guest, the moment he tasted the cakes, drop down on all fours and begin to bray. Each had turned into a fine strong donkey; and the hostess forthwith drove them into her stable, and took possession of their belongings.

Chao did not tell a soul about his adventure; but a month later, when his business in Lo Yang was finished, he returned, and stopped one evening at the 'Footbridge Tavern'. He had with him some fresh buckwheat cakes, of the same size and shape as those made at the time of his former visit by Mrs Number Three.

The inn appeared to be empty, and she made him very comfortable. Before he went to bed, she asked him if he wished to order anything.

'Not tonight,' he replied, 'but I should like something to eat first thing in the morning, before I go.'

'You shall have a good meal,' said the hostess.

During the night, the usual magic growth of buckwheat took place, and the next morning she placed before Chao a dish of buckwheat cakes. While she was away for a few minutes, Chao took one of the magic cakes off the dish, replaced it by one of his own, and waited for her to return. When she came back, she said, 'You are not eating anything.'

'I was waiting for you,' he replied. 'I have some cakes. If you will not try one of mine, I shall not eat those you have given me.'

'Give me one,' said Mrs Number Three.

Chao handed her the magic cake he had taken from the dish, and the moment she put her teeth into it she went down on all fours and began to bray. She had become a fine strong she-ass.

Chao harnessed her, and rode home on her back, taking with him the box of wooden figures; but as he did not know the spell, he was unable to make them move, or to turn other people into asses.

Mrs Number Three was the strongest and most enduring donkey imaginable. She could travel 100 li a day on any road.

Four years later, Chao was riding her past a temple dedicated to Mount Hua, when an old man suddenly began clapping his hands and laughing, crying out, 'Now, Mrs Number Three of the Footbridge, what's happened to you, eh?' Then, seizing the bridle, he said to Chao, 'She has tried to do you a wrong, I grant, but she has now performed sufficient penance for her sins. Let me now set her free!' Then he took the halter off her head, and immediately she shed the ass's skin and stood upright in human form. She saluted the old man and vanished. No one has ever heard of her since.

Reading for meaning

As you read the story, consider the following questions:

1   Which country is this story from? What are the clues that tell you this? List all the clues you can find.

2   What initial impression do you form of Mrs Number Three? When does your opinion of her start to change?

3   What reasons does the traveller have for tricking Mrs Number Three?

4   a)   Who is the old man that releases her from the spell?

   b)   Why do you think he releases her?

5   Why do you think Mrs Number Three never re-appears?

Sentences, paragraphs and punctuation

There are two main sentence types: **simple** and **complex**. A **simple sentence** contains one main idea. For example: 'They came to life.' A **complex sentence** contains more than one idea and can be made up of several clauses. For example: 'Before he went to bed, she asked him if he wished to order anything.' One clause will be the **main clause** that will deal with the main idea of the sentence. There will also be at least one **subordinate clause** that gives extra information.

For example:
'When the ploughing was done, (subordinate clause)

she handed the drover a packet of buckwheat grains'. (main clause)

The subordinate clause adds more meaning to the main clause of the complex sentence.

1 Write this complex sentence as four simple sentences:

'While she was away for a few minutes, Chao took one of the magic cakes off the dish, replaced it by one of his own, and waited for her to return.'

2 Highlight the punctuation marks used and explain their purpose in the following sentence:

'It was a comfortable, roomy inn; the hostess was in easy circumstances, and had a herd of very fine asses.'

Writing to analyse, review and comment

Write three paragraphs which:

- **review** the story, highlighting its most interesting and unusual aspects

- **comment** on how the central female protagonist is presented. For example: vulnerable; in need of help; a cunning and devious schemer; a beautiful but silly girl

- **analyse** why you enjoyed reading this story. Is it the storyline, the characters, the setting, the writer's style?

Days of chivalry

Arthurian legend

One of the most famous stories of honour and chivalry is the legend of King Arthur and his Knights of the Round Table. King Arthur and his Queen, Guinevere, set up court in the magical castle of Camelot. Their faithful knights, who swore to defend all against the forces of evil, attended them. The tales of their deeds of courage and daring are too many to mention. Sir Lancelot was the most famous knight. He was renowned for his bravery and courage on the battlefield.

Le Morte D'Arthur

"What would ye that I did?" said Sir Lancelot.
"I would have you to my husband," said Elaine.
"Fair damsel, I thank you," said Sir Lancelot,
"but truly," said he, "I cast me never to be wedded man."
"Then, fair knight," said she, "will ye be my paramour?"
"Jesu defend me," said Sir Lancelot, "for then I
rewarded your father and your brother full evil
for their great goodness."
"Alas," said she, "then must I die for your love."

Book XVIII Chap. XIX.

Reading for meaning

1   What vow has Sir Lancelot made to the damsel Elaine? Use quotation from the extract to support your answer.

2   What are Elaine's feelings for Sir Lancelot? Support your answer with quotation.

Archaic language differs from **standard English** in two ways, the type of vocabulary used and the manner in which the sentences are constructed. Often, the words used are unfamiliar and the order in which these words are organised is different from the order we use today. For example: 'I cast me never to be a wedded man.'

Standard English is the accepted language of public communication, which follows commonly accepted conventions of vocabulary choice, spelling, punctuation and grammar.

3   a)   What do you notice about the way the sentences are constructed in this extract?

     b)   How does it differ from the way you might construct a sentence?

4   Rewrite the conversation in **modern English**, keeping the original meaning intact.

The next piece of writing is taken from the poem called 'The Ballad of Elaine' by Sydney Fowler Wright. In this poem, Wright describes the meeting between Elaine and Sir Lancelot.

The Ballad of Elaine

She came when evening came, – her feet
The cool grass comforted, –
Where love through morn and noon-day heat
Her seeking steps had led
To him who had no love for her,   5
And nigh whose life was dead.

Lone through the lengthened days he lay
Within that hermit's cave,
Since, on the fatal tourney day,
So deep the lancehead drave   10
It seemed nor any skill could heal,
Nor any love could save.

Was closed that riven hurt where – through
The restless life had drained.
No more the aching wound he knew,   15
No more its healing pained.
Quiet in the shadowed cave he lay,
As one whose goal was gained.

Only he would for speech with him
To whom in life he clave,   20
The good knight Bors, whose lance too well
That wound unweening gave,
That he might ere his parting tell
How well his heart forgave.

"Damsel, my space of days is sped,   25
    I wot God's night is near,
But could'st thou hold my life," he said,
    "Till that good knight is here,
You might not ask so great a thing
    That you should ask in fear."   30

"I'll ask one boon of God's Mother,
    Ere aught I'll ask of thee.
I'll ask one gift of God's Mother,
    That she should grant it me,
Though needly at the feet of God   35
    She lay my life in fee."

She searched that closing wound anew,
    Its utter depth she learned.
She dressed it with the skill she knew,
    With herbs that waked and burned,   40
Till where the dying life withdrew
    Its aching pain returned.

The changing day was night without,
    The changing night was day.
Through the long hours with life in doubt   45
    In ever pain he lay.
Only the weary day was night:
    Only the night was day.

And still her constant watch she kept,
    And gained nor glance nor word,   50
And still her constant prayer she wept
    Till Mary Virgin heard,
And then in quiet ease he slept,
    And then from sleep he stirred.

The Ballad of Elaine

> A **ballad** is a poem, sometimes set to music as a song, which tells a story. The stanzas are usually quite short, with a simple rhythm and rhyme scheme. There may be a lot of repetition, for example, of words or phrases, or even of a whole stanza that is used as a chorus or to remind you of the subject of the poem. Many ballads are based on actual events and people, although there are often imaginative additions or changes to the original details.

Reading for meaning

1 What had happened to Sir Lancelot?

2 What do we learn about Elaine's skills?

3 Why does Sir Lancelot want Elaine to help him?

4 How does Elaine feel about Sir Lancelot? Select one phrase that clearly shows the depth of her feelings.

Ballads

1 In what ways does this poem conform to the definitions of a ballad? Use reference from the text to support your answer.

2 Sydney Fowler Wright uses an example of **personification** in the opening stanza of the poem. Find this example and explain why he has chosen to use this particular expression.

3 One common feature of ballads is the use of archaic words and phrases. Find three examples in this text and explain what they mean.

In this next poem, Alfred, Lord Tennyson is writing about the same damsel, Elaine of Estolat. As you read the poem, note any similarities and differences between this story and 'The Ballad of Elaine'.

The Lady of Shalott

PART I

On either side the river lie
Long fields of barley and of rye,
That clothe the wold and meet the sky;
And thro' the field the road runs by
To many-tower'd Camelot;   5
And up and down the people go,
Gazing where the lilies blow
Round an island there below,
The island of Shalott.

Willows whiten, aspens quiver,   10
Little breezes dusk and shiver
Thro' the wave that runs for ever
By the island in the river
Flowing down to Camelot.
Four gray walls, and four gray towers,   15
Overlook a space of flowers,
And the silent isle imbowers
The Lady of Shalott.

By the margin, willow veil'd,
Slide the heavy barges trail'd   20
By slow horses; and unhail'd
The shallop flitteth silken-sail'd
Skimming down to Camelot:
But who hath seen her wave her hand?
Or at the casement seen her stand?   25
Or is she known in all the land,
    The Lady of Shalott?

Only reapers, reaping early
In among the bearded barley,
Hear a song that echoes cheerly   30
From the river winding clearly,
    Down to tower'd Camelot:
And by the moon the reaper weary,
Piling sheaves in uplands airy,
Listening, "whispers 'Tis the fairy   35
    Lady of Shalott."

PART II

There she weaves by night and day
A magic web with colours gay.
She has heard a whisper say,
A curse is on her if she stay   40
    To look down to Camelot.
She knows not what the curse may be,
And so she weaveth steadily,
And little other care hath she,
    The Lady of Shalott.   45

And moving thro' a mirror clear
That hangs before her all the year,
Shadows of the world appear.
There she sees the highway near
    Winding down to Camelot: 50

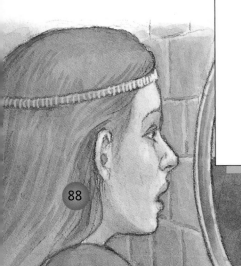

There the river eddy whirls,
And there the surly village-churls,
And the red cloaks of market girls,
Pass onward from Shalott.

Sometimes a troop of damsels glad,   55
An abbot on an ambling pad,
Sometimes a curly shepherd-lad,
Or long-hair'd page in crimson clad,
Goes by to tower'd Camelot;
And sometimes thro' the mirror blue   60
The knights come riding two and two:
She hath no loyal knight and true,
The Lady of Shalott.

But in her web she still delights
To weave the mirror's magic sights,   65
For often thro' the silent nights
A funeral, with plumes and lights
And music, went to Camelot:
Or when the moon was overhead,
Came two young lovers lately wed: 70
"I am half sick of shadows," said
The Lady of Shalott.

PART III

A bow-shot from her bower-eaves,
He rode between the barley-sheaves,
The sun came dazzling thro' the leaves,   75
And flamed upon the brazen greaves
Of bold Sir Lancelot.
A red-cross knight for ever kneel'd
To a lady in his shield,
That sparkled on the yellow field,   80
Beside remote Shalott.

The gemmy bridle glitter'd free,
Like to some branch of stars we see
Hung in the golden Galaxy.
The bridle bells rang merrily   85
As he rode down to Camelot:
And from his blazon'd baldric slung
A mighty silver bugle hung,
And as he rode his armour rung,
      Beside remote Shalott.   90

All in the blue unclouded weather
Thick-jewell'd shone the saddle-leather,
The helmet and the helmet-feather
Burn'd like one burning flame together,
      As he rode down to Camelot.   95
As often thro' the purple night,
Below the starry clusters bright,
Some bearded meteor, trailing light,
      Moves over still Shalott.

His broad clear brow in sunlight glow'd;   100
On burnish'd hooves his war-horse trode;
From underneath his helmet flow'd
His coal-black curls as on he rode,
      As he rode down to Camelot.
From the bank and from the river   105
He flash'd into the crystal mirror,
      "Tirra lirra," by the river
      Sang Sir Lancelot.

She left the web, she left the loom,
She made three paces thro' the room,   110
She saw the water-lily bloom,
She saw the helmet and the plume,
      She look'd down to Camelot.
Out flew the web and floated wide;

The mirror crack'd from side to side;   115
"The curse is come upon me," cried
The Lady of Shalott.

PART IV

In the stormy east-wind straining,
The pale yellow woods were waning,
The broad stream in his banks complaining,   120
Heavily the low sky raining
Over tower'd Camelot;
Down she came and found a boat
Beneath a willow left afloat,
And round about the prow she wrote   125
The Lady of Shalott.

And down the river's dim expanse
Like some bold seer in a trance,
Seeing all his own mischance –
With a glassy countenance   130
Did she look to Camelot
And at the closing of the day
She loosed the chain, and down she lay;
The broad stream bore her far away,
The Lady of Shalott.   135

Lying, robed in snowy white
That loosely flew to left and right –
The leaves upon her falling light –
Thro' the noises of the night
She floated down to Camelot: 140
And as the boat-head wound along
The willowy hills and fields among,
They heard her singing her last song,
The Lady of Shalott.

Heard a carol, mournful, holy,   145
Chanted loudly, chanted lowly,
Till her blood was frozen slowly,
And her eyes were darken'd wholly,
Turn'd to tower'd Camelot.
For ere she reach'd upon the tide   150
The first house by the water-side,
Singing in her song she died,
The Lady of Shalott.

Under tower and balcony,
By garden-wall and gallery,   155
A gleaming shape she floated by,
Dead-pale between the houses high,
Silent into Camelot.
Out upon the wharfs they came,
Knight and burgher, lord and dame,   160
And round the prow they read her name,
The Lady of Shalott.

Who is this? and what is here?
And in the lighted palace near
Died the sound of royal cheer;   165
And they cross'd themselves for fear,
All the knights at Camelot:
But Lancelot mused a little space;
He said, "She has a lovely face;
God in his mercy lend her grace,   170
The Lady of Shalott."

Reading for meaning

1 In Part I, Tennyson describes the setting of this story.

   a) What picture of the countryside does he create? How does he create this picture?

   b) How is the Lady of Shalott's house described in comparison with this scene? What is the effect of this description?

2 The 'reapers' only 'hear a song that echoes cheerily' and whisper " 'Tis the fairy Lady of Shalott." Why do the reapers know nothing of this Lady? *Hint: Read Part II.*

3 How does the Lady of Shalott feel about her situation? How do you know this?

4 Part III of the poem introduces the character of Sir Lancelot.

   a) How does Tennyson describe Sir Lancelot?

   b) What impression of Sir Lancelot does he want to convey? Use supporting quotation in your answer.

5 The sight of Lancelot has a dramatic effect on the Lady of Shalott.

   a) What happens?

   b) What does this have in common with the story Sidney Fowler Wright tells in the previous extract?

The Lady of Shalott by John W. Waterhouse

Alfred, Lord Tennyson's poetic technique

1 Tennyson has used repetition throughout the poem. Find examples of repetition in the text and explain what different purposes and effects they achieve.

2 Why does the poem have such a regular rhythm and rhyme scheme?

3 Tennyson uses sounds to great effect in this poem. Select five examples of **alliteration** and/or **assonance** and explain your reasons for choice, including an explanation of the effect achieved.

4 a) In what ways does the mood change in Part IV?

   b) How does Tennyson achieve this change in mood?

Writing to persuade, argue and advise

Having read the versions of this story and collected information about Sir Lancelot, write an editorial for a tabloid newspaper, entitled:

'Sir Lancelot – giant or gigolo?'

In the article, you will need to use the following techniques that are characteristic of editorial writing.

Editorials:
- are often short and 'punchy' in style
- present one point of view
- are written with a sense of conviction
- persuade the reader
- use facts and quotations from reliable sources
- develop an argument in a reasoned manner
- use discourse markers, for example, 'but', 'therefore', 'despite this', 'whilst'
- have a conclusion which poses a question or calls for action.

2.5   Good over evil

Star Wars – The Empire Strikes Back

Luke has landed on the planet Dagobah in his search for the Jedi Master. The Jedi Master will teach Luke the skills he needs to become a full Jedi Knight, ready to take on the power of Darth Vader and the evil Emperor. The following extracts are taken from the film script.

The Empire Strikes Back

Interior

Creature's house

> Artoo, peeking in the window, sees the inside of the house – a very plain, but cozy dwelling. Everything is the same small scale as the creature. The only thing out of place in the miniature room is Luke, whose height makes the four-foot ceiling seem even lower. He sits cross-legged on the floor of the living room. The creature is in an adjoining area – his little kitchen – cooking up an incredible meal. The stove is a steaming hodge-podge of pots and pans. The wizened little host scurries about chopping this, shredding that, and showering everything with exotic herbs and spices. He rushes back and forth putting platters on the table in front of Luke, who watches the creature impatiently...

LUKE: How far away is Yoda? Will it take us long to get there?

CREATURE: Not far. Yoda not far. Patience. Soon you will be with him. (tasting food from the pot) Rootleaf, I cook. Why wish you become Jedi? Hm?

LUKE: Mostly because of my father, I guess.

CREATURE: Ah, your father. Powerful Jedi was he, powerful Jedi, mmm.

LUKE: (a little angry) Oh, come on. How could you know my father? You don't even know who I am. (fed up) Oh, I don't even know what I'm doing here. We're wasting our time. *The creature turns away from Luke and speaks to a third party.*

CREATURE: (irritated) I cannot teach him. The boy has no patience. *Luke's head spins in the direction the creature faces. But there is no one there. The boy is bewildered, but it gradually dawns on him that the little creature is Yoda, the Jedi Master, and that he is speaking with Ben.*

BEN'S VOICE: He will learn patience.

YODA: Hmmm. Much anger in him, like his father.

BEN'S VOICE: Was I any different when you taught me?

YODA: Hah. He is not ready.

LUKE: Yoda! I am ready. I...Ben! I can be a Jedi. Ben, tell him I'm ready. *Trying to see Ben, Luke starts to get up but hits his head on the low ceiling.*

YODA: Ready, are you? What know you of ready? For eight hundred years have I trained Jedi. My own counsel will I keep on who is to be trained! A Jedi must have the deepest commitment, the most serious mind. (to the invisible Ben, indicating Luke) This one a long time have I watched. Never his mind on where he was. Hmm? What he was doing. Hmph. Adventure. Heh! Excitement. Heh! A Jedi craves not these things. (turning to Luke) You are reckless! *Luke looks down. He knows it is true.*

BEN'S VOICE: So was I, if you'll remember.

YODA: He is too old. Yes, too old to begin the training. *Luke thinks he detects a subtle softening in Yoda's voice.*

LUKE: But I've learned so much. *Yoda turns his piercing gaze on Luke, as though the Jedi Master's huge eyes could somehow determine how much the boy had learned. After a long moment, the little Jedi turns toward where he alone sees Ben.*

YODA: (sighs) Will he finished what he begins?

LUKE: I won't fail you – I'm not afraid.

YODA: (turns slowly toward him) Oh, you will be. You will be.

Reading for meaning

1 a) What is your first impression of Luke in this scene? What evidence leads you to assume this?

   b) Why does Yoda doubt Luke's ability?

2 Luke does not expect Yoda to be the Jedi teacher he has come to find. Why not?

3 With this start, how successful do you think their relationship will be?

Exterior

Dagobah – day

> With Yoda strapped to his back, Luke climbs up one of the many thick vines that grow in the swamp. Panting heavily, he continues his course –- climbing, flipping through the air, jumping over roots, and racing in and out of the heavy ground fog.

YODA: Run! Yes. A Jedi's strength flows from the Force. But beware of the dark side. Anger...fear...aggression. The dark side of the Force are they. Easily they flow, quick to join you in a fight. If once you start down the dark path, forever will it dominate your destiny, consume you it will, as it did Obi-Wan's apprentice.

LUKE: Vader. Is the dark side stronger?

YODA: No...no...no. Quicker, easier, more seductive.

LUKE: But how am I to know the good side from the bad?

YODA: You will know. When you are calm, at peace. Passive. A Jedi uses the Force for knowledge and defense, never for attack.

LUKE: But tell me why I can't...

YODA: (interrupting) No, no, there is no why. Nothing more will I teach you today. Clear your mind of questions. Mmm. Mmmmmm.

Artoo beeps in the distance as Luke lets Yoda down to the ground. Breathing heavily, he takes his shirt from a nearby tree branch and pulls it on. He turns to see a huge, dead, black tree, its base surrounded by a few feet of water. Giant, twisted roots form a dark and sinister cave on one side. Luke stares at the tree, trembling.

LUKE: There's something not right here. I feel cold, death.

YODA: That place...is strong with the dark side of the Force. A domain of evil it is. In you must go.

LUKE: What's in there?

YODA: Only what you take with you. *Luke looks warily between the tree and Yoda. He starts to strap on his weapon belt.*

YODA: Your weapons...you will not need them. *Luke gives the tree a long look, then shakes his head "no". Yoda shrugs. Luke reaches up to brush aside some hanging vines and enters the tree.*

Reading for meaning

In order to make the film script exciting and hold the audience's attention, a number of dramatic techniques are used. These include:

- adding moments of tension when the audience does not know what is about to happen

- creating a change of mood or pace between scenes

- using a narrator to add insight into the character's feelings.

1 List the words and phrases used to create the atmosphere of suspense before Luke enters the root cave and explain why they build tension.

2 What other dramatic techniques are employed to make this scene tense and exciting? Explain these techniques in detail and give supporting quotation where appropriate.

Standard English and language variation

1 a) What is unusual about the manner in which Yoda speaks?

b) In what way does it differ from **standard English**?

c) Give three examples of this unusual use of language.

d) How would you adjust these examples to make them standard English?

Exterior

Dagobah – bog – day

Luke's face is upside-down and showing enormous strain. He stands on his hands, with Yoda perched on his feet. Opposite Luke and Yoda are two rocks the size of bowling balls. Luke stares at the rocks and concentrates. One of the rocks lifts from the ground and floats up to rest on the other.

YODA: Use the Force. Yes... *Yoda taps Luke's leg. Quickly, Luke lifts one hand from the ground. His body wavers, but he maintains his balance. Artoo, standing nearby, is whistling and beeping frantically.*

YODA: Now...the stone. Feel it. *Luke concentrates on trying to lift the top rock. It rises a few feet, shaking under the strain. But, distracted by Artoo's frantic beeping, Luke loses his balance and finally collapses. Yoda jumps clear.*

YODA: Concentrate! *Annoyed at the disturbance, Luke looks over at Artoo, who is rocking urgently back and forth in front of him. Artoo waddles closer to Luke, chirping wildly, then scoots over the edge of the swamp. Catching on, Luke rushes to the water's edge. The X-wing fighter has sunk, and only the tip of its nose shows above the lake's surface.*

LUKE: Oh, no. We'll never get it out now. *Yoda stamps his foot in irritation.*

YODA: So certain are you. Always with you it cannot be done. Hear you nothing that I say? *Luke looks uncertainly out at the ship.*

LUKE: Master, moving stones around is one thing. This is totally different.

YODA: No! No different! Only different in your mind. You must unlearn what you have learned.

LUKE: (focusing, quietly) All right, I'll give it a try.

YODA: No! Try not. Do. Or do not. There is no try. *Luke closes his eyes and concentrates on thinking the ship out. Slowly, the X-wing's nose begins to rise above the water. It hovers for a moment and then slides back, disappearing once again.*

LUKE: (panting heavily) I can't. It's too big.

YODA: Size matters not. Look at me. Judge me by my size, do you? Hm? Mmmm. *Luke shakes his head.*

YODA: And well you should not. For my ally is the Force. And a powerful ally it is. Life creates it, makes it grow. Its energy surrounds us and binds us. Luminous beings are we...(Yoda pinches Luke's shoulder)...not this crude matter. (a sweeping gesture) You must feel the Force around you. (gesturing) Here, between you...me...the tree...the rock...everywhere! Yes, even between this land and that ship!

LUKE: (discouraged) You want the impossible. *Quietly Yoda turns toward the X-wing fighter. With his eyes closed and his head bowed, he raises his arm and points at the ship. Soon, the fighter rises above the water and moves forward as Artoo beeps in terror and scoots away. The entire*

X-wing moves majestically, surely, toward the shore. Yoda stands on a tree root and guides the fighter carefully down toward the beach. Luke stares in astonishment as the fighter settles down onto the shore. He walks toward Yoda.

LUKE: I don't...I don't believe it.

YODA: That is why you fail. *Luke shakes his head, bewildered.*

Exterior

Dagobah – bog – clearing day

In the clearing behind Yoda's house, Luke again stands upside-down, but his face shows less strain and more concentration than before. Yoda sits on the ground below the young warrior. On the other side of the clearing, two equipment cases slowly rise into the air. Nearby Artoo watches, humming to himself, when suddenly he, too, rises into the air. His little legs kick desperately and his head turns frantically, looking for help.

YODA: Concentrate...feel the Force flow. Yes. Good. Calm, yes. Through the Force, things you will see. Other places. The future...the past. Old friends long gone. *Luke suddenly becomes distressed.*

LUKE: Han! Leia! *The two packing boxes and Artoo fall to the ground with a crash, then Luke himself tumbles over.*

YODA: (shaking his head) Hmm. Control, control. You must learn control.

LUKE: I saw...I saw a city in the clouds.

YODA: Mmm. Friends you have there.

LUKE: They were in pain.

YODA: It is the future you see.

LUKE: Future? Will they die? *Yoda closes his eyes and lowers his head.*

YODA: Difficult to see. Always in motion is the future.

LUKE: I've got to go to them.

YODA: Decide you must how to serve them best. If you leave now, help them you could. But you would destroy all for which they have fought and suffered. *Luke is stopped cold by Yoda's words. Gloom shrouds him as he nods his head sadly.*

Reading for meaning

1 Having read the complete extract, what do you think Luke has learned by the time he has to leave?

2 Why do you think he decides to go rather than stay and complete his training? What does Yoda think he should do? How do we know this?

3 The Jedi get their power from the Force. What is the Force and what powers does it give the Jedi Knight?

4 What is the **philosophy** of the Jedi Knight? (Investigate the meaning of this term before you answer the question. Discuss the meaning as a class.)

5 Once Luke leaves Dagobah, he will be alone. Is this true? Explain your answer.

Writing to inform, explain and describe

Luke is on Dagobah to learn how to become a Jedi Knight. Yoda is his 'personal trainer'. Using the information in the text about the skills required to be a Jedi Knight, devise Luke's training schedule for a week. You should present your information in a clear manner that is easy to read and understand.

Review

What did you particularly enjoy in this chapter?

What did you not like very much?

Was there anything:

- you found difficult to understand?

- you discovered or understood for the first time?

Use this checklist to help you answer these questions and to review the progress you have made.

- **You have read:** an extract from a novel; a short story from another culture; a piece of non-fiction (press release); an extract from a classic Greek tale by Homer, 'The Odyssey'; poetry from pre-1914 and one poem written recently; an extract from a film.

- **You have thought about how writers use:** traditional and modern poetic structure; technical devices such as personification and assonance, rhyme and rhythm; words and phrases to create mood; narrative viewpoint; dramatic techniques; language and presentational devices in information texts.

- **You have written to:** inform, explain, describe – an extract from a travel guide, instructions for a character to follow, a training schedule; persuade, argue, advise – an editorial; imagine, explore, entertain – a poem; analyse, review, comment – two responses to text.

- **To improve your writing you have thought about:** word families; spelling of unusual words; the use of contractions or elided words; using wordbanks to help you describe vividly; the use of different types of sentences to achieve effect; repetition and how this can be used to create a mood or an atmosphere; connecting sentences in various ways; humour.

- **Your speaking and listening work has included:** paired and group discussion of ideas and issues; an activity in which you have assumed the role of a character from a text; performing a scene from a play; evaluating your own and others' work.

- **You may have used ICT to:** research information on a number of topics; spellcheck and present your final drafts neatly and attractively.

3 Our world

This chapter is about our world: the children who live in it, the extreme places we can find in it and the creatures that share it with us. You will read, write, speak and think about a range of ideas such as:

- how children interact with the world around them
- what life is like at the 'end of the world', the South Pole
- what the lives of some of the most unpopular creatures in our world are like.

3.1 Poetry and fiction – children at play

Children's Games

The modern American poet William Carlos Williams wrote this poem, entitled 'Children's Games', after he had seen a painting by the sixteenth century Flemish artist Pieter Bruegel. You can see the painting on page 110.

Before you read

1   In groups, brainstorm a list of games you played as young children in the playground, park or garden. As a class, list them on the board.

2   Discuss the class list of games. How, if at all, do these relate to the adult world?

As you read

1   On a spider diagram, record the different kinds of game played in the poem.

2   Write down any old-fashioned words or phrases that show the scene Williams describes is not modern. For example: 'hogshead'.

Children's Games

Part I

This is a schoolyard
crowded
with children

of all ages near a village
on a small stream   5
meandering by

where some boys
are swimming
bare-ass

or climbing a tree in leaf   10
everything
is motion

elder women are looking
after the small
fry   15

a play wedding a
christening
nearby one leans

hollering
into   20
an empty hogshead

Part II

Little girls
whirling their skirts about
until they stand out flat

tops pinwheels   25
to run in the wind with
or a toy in 3 tiers to spin

with a piece
of twine to make it go
blindman's-buff follow the   30

leader stilts
high and low tipcat jacks
bowls hanging by the knees

standing on your head
run the gauntlet   35
a dozen on their backs

feet together kicking
through which a boy must pass
roll the hoop or a

construction   40
made of bricks
some mason has abandoned

Part III

The desperate toys
of children
their   45

imagination equilibrium
and rocks
which are to be

found
everywhere   50
and games to drag
the other down
blindfold
to make use of

a swinging   55
weight
with which

at random
to bash in the
heads about   60

them
Brueghel saw it all
and with his grim

humor faithfully
recorded   65
it

Reading for meaning

1 Write down two things you notice about the poem.

2 Describe the form the poem is written in. What effect have the lack of punctuation, rhyme and capital letters?

3 a) Make a list of the verbs used to describe the children at play. Why does the writer choose these particular words?

   b) The verbs, like 'climbing' are, in the present tense. Why do you think Williams chooses the present tense?

Language is the words the poet has chosen and why.
Style is the way the poem is written or organised.
Themes are what the poet has written about.

Commas are used to separate the **phrases** or **clauses** within a sentence, and **semi-colons** are used when you want a clearer break than a comma, but not a **full stop**. For example: 'Boys and girls played, but not together; boys hurtled like pinballs from wall to wall, fighting with light-sabres; girls linked arms and cantered.'

---

4 Explain how Williams uses the poetic techniques of onomatopoeia and alliteration.

5 Make a grid, like the one below, and write six statements about the way children's games are described in the poem, selecting a quotation to support your comment in each case. For example: purpose built toys, objects not seen as toys, specific games with rules.

Statement about the children's games	Quotation from the poem
Some of the games imitate things that happen in the adult world	'a play wedding a christening'

'Children's Games', by Pieter Breugel

111

Drama

1 a) In groups of four, make six **tableaux** (or freeze frames) that demonstrate what your group thinks are the six most important moments from the poem.

 b) Give each tableau a caption or title, which should be a line from the text.

2 Ensure each person in the group is in at least one tableau. Choose one person to read out the captions. Count down from three into each of your tableaux. Make the transitions between tableaux smooth by 'freezing' and 'melting'.

> **Tableaux** can also be called freeze frames, stills or statues, which are like photographs that have been taken of a series of moments from a drama.

Writing to describe

1 Look at Breugel's painting 'Children's Games' (on the previous pages), which inspired Williams' poem, and try to find each description of the children at play from the poem in the picture.

2 Write an imaginary description of a busy, modern playground.

 ● Think of modern games.

 ● Choose language that shows how new technology has changed children's games. For example: you might describe children playing with hand-held computer games, mobile phones, or play-fighting with space age weapons.

 ● Organise your description in paragraphs, and think carefully about your sentence punctuation.

 ● Include colours, sound effects, movements, details from the games, the children's reactions, the presence of any adults.

3 Once you have finished, read through and check. Pay particular attention to paragraphing and sentence construction.

 You could present your description with an illustration, for display.

3.2 At the end of the world

In this section you will read two different **non-fiction** texts. Both are written to inform you about the areas known as the 'ends of the Earth': the North and South Polar regions. The first text draws a direct comparison between the North and South Poles, and the second is an extract from a travel journal. Both books are called 'Pole to Pole'.

Before you read

Brainstorm everything you know about the North and South Poles. You could think about:

- the geography
- the weather
- historical adventures
- wildlife
- climate change.

Pole to Pole 1

As you read

1 As you read this extract from 'Pole to Pole', look closely at the way the page is set out. What do you notice about the layout?

2 Think about the effectiveness of the presentation; how many different images are there? How are the images different from each other?

3 How many different sections of text are there? Why do you think there are so many? Is this a good thing, do you think?

THE SOUTH POLE

T he South Pole lies in the middle of the continent of Antarctica – the name means 'opposite the Arctic'. Antarctica is a mountainous continent that is almost completely covered by a gigantic ice sheet and is the size of Europe and the USA put together. Unlike the Arctic, the Antarctic has very little ice-free land, even in summer. It has no land mammals and fewer plants and animals than the Arctic.

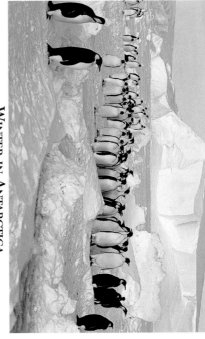

WINTER IN ANTARCTICA

Penguins live only in the southern half of the world, mainly in and around Antarctica, so polar bears and penguins never meet. Only two species of penguin, the Adélie and the emperor, breed on the Antarctic continent itself. Most penguins leap ashore to breed during the summer, but the emperor penguin (as seen here) lays its eggs in the winter. This allows the chick to hatch in early spring and have the whole summer to grow.

ANTARCTIC FLOWERS

Only two flowering plants grow on Antarctica and neither of them looks much like a flowering plant because they have tiny, drab-coloured flowers. The most common is Antarctic hairgrass (above) and the other is a type of pearlwort called *Colobanthus*.

THE ANTARCTIC ICE

The Antarctic continent is almost completely covered by a gigantic ice sheet, up to 4 km (2.5 miles) thick.

WEST

If the ice was removed the land would rise about 550 metres (1,800 ft).

A few mountains, called nunataks, extend their peak above the ice.

More than half of the surface of Antarctica lies below sea level.

EAST

THE ANTARCTIC

The Antarctic region is separated from the rest of the world by the stormy waters of the Southern Ocean. In winter, ice extends hundreds of kilometres out into the ocean from Antarctic coasts. There are several groups of remote islands near Antarctica (such as South Georgia), but the nearest landmass is the southern tip of South America, which is about 960 km (600 miles) away. On maps, the Antarctic region is bordered by an imaginary line called the Antarctic Circle.

THE NORTH POLE

Although the areas around the North Pole and the South Pole are both cold places and home to many similar animals, they have a very different geography. The North pole lies in the middle of a shallow, frozen ocean surrounded by the northern edges of Europe, Asia and North America. This whole area is called Arctic, named after Arktos, the Great Bear Star constellation, which dominated the northern polar skies.

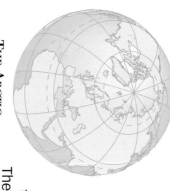

THE ARCTIC

The Arctic region consists mainly of the Arctic Ocean, which can be as much as 1,600 km (1,000 miles) across and has a thin skin of ice on top. The largest island in the Arctic Ocean is Greenland, which is covered in a thick ice sheet. Also part of the Arctic is a band of land called the tundra, which means 'treeless land'. This covers the northern parts of Canada, Alaska, Russia and Scandinavia. On maps, an imaginary line called the Arctic Circle surrounds the Arctic area.

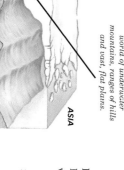

NORTH AMERICA

ASIA

THE ARCTIC ICE

The middle of the Arctic is frozen all year round, although the ice is less than 10 metres (33 ft) thick.

In winter, the ice covers an area 1 1/2 times the size of Canada, but the edges melt in summer.

The sea bed is a pitch-dark world of underwater mountains, ranges of hills and vast, flat plains.

LIVING IN THE ARCTIC

Polar bears are the only animals to live and hunt on top of the Arctic Ocean – polar bear tracks have even been found near the North Pole itself. There are probably about 20,000 polar bear wandering along over the remote Arctic ice floes as they hunt for seals beneath the ice.

ARCTIC FLOWERS

The tundra landscape is low and flat, with no trees, but many low bushes, lichens, mosses and grasses. In summer, parts of the tundra burst into bloom as flowering plants rush to flower and produce seeds before the short spell of warm weather ends. There are over 500 species of flowering plants in the Arctic.

Reading for meaning

1 Look at the table below. In the left-hand column you can see features typical of the **genre** of information writing. These common aspects of the text are called **stylistic conventions**.

2 Re-read the text, fill in the table below, and analyse the ways in which the writer has used the stylistic conventions of information writing.

Stylistic Convention	Example(s)	Explanation/ Analysis
Headings and sub-headings	'The North Pole' 'Antarctic flowers'	Headings and sub-headings help to structure the information into categories, and make it clearer, and easier to understand
Technical or specialist vocabulary	'the tundra' 'a few mountains called nunataks'	
Facts and statistics		
Use of the present tense		
Diagrams and maps		
Photographic images		

The word **genre** describes different types of writing with their own characteristics or features. For example: crime writing, historical novels, or information writing. The **present tense** is used in information writing to pass on information about the way something *is*. For example: 'The South Pole *lies* in the middle of the continent of Antarctica.'

Spelling and vocabulary

The text you have just read tells us that the word 'Antarctica' means 'opposite the Arctic'.

There are two similar-sounding **prefixes** that have different meanings and which are both like the sound at the beginning of the word '**An**tarctica'. These are:

• **Ante**, which means 'before' or 'previous to'

• **Anti**, which means 'opposite' or 'against'

Collect as many different words as you can which begin with either **prefix**. Then look in a dictionary to check and complete your lists.

Writing to compare

1 Re-read the texts 'The North Pole' and 'The South Pole'. Try to find as many differences as you can between the Arctic and the Antarctic.

2 Collect your ideas in columns, adding 'areas for contrast' for example: animal life, geographical features, location, the names and their meanings.

3 a) Write a comparison between 'The North Pole' and 'The South Pole'. Write a paragraph for each area of contrast that you found.

   b) Link your sentences together by using some of these **connectives of contrast**: whereas, instead of, alternatively, otherwise, unlike, on the other hand.

Connectives are words and short phrases which link ideas to make our writing more cohesive. For example: 'The North Pole lies in the middle of a shallow, frozen ocean surrounded by the northern edges of Europe, Asia and North America, **whereas** the South Pole lies in the middle of the continent of Antarctica.' This is a **connective of contrast**, because it helps us to contrast the two ideas.

Pole to Pole 2

The following extracts are the final two chapters of Michael Palin's account 'Pole To Pole', which was about his voyage around the world starting at the North Pole and finishing at the South Pole. Day 140 and Day 141 trace the final stage of his journey, and feature his arrival at the South Pole.

As you read

Think about the differences between the normal morning routine in your house, and the routine described by Michael Palin in 'Day 140'.

- Write a series of descriptions to show the sequence of events after Michael Palin wakens until the go-ahead is given for loading the plane. Contrast these with what happens in your home.

Sequence of event	Description of events in your household	Description of event in 'Day 140'
Waking up	'I am woken up by my alarm clock'	He is woken by the sound of the polar wind
Getting dressed		
Washing		
Looking in the mirror		

DAY 140 · PATRIOT HILLS TO THE THIEL MOUNTAINS

Wake from utterly warm, comfortable, womb-like night, curled up half-dressed inside my RAB sleeping-bag, to the desolate sound of a polar wind, sighing, hissing, slapping at the sides of the tent like some irascible neighbour. As if pleased with itself for having at last woken me it seems to grow in intensity. Look around the tent. Fraser is invisible – somewhere in his sleeping-bag I presume, Clem snores reassuringly, as I feel he might do if the battle of Waterloo were being fought outside, Basil, his face masked against the daylight, looks like a cross between a bank robber and someone halfway through cosmetic surgery. Nigel lies awake, probably wondering, like me, if this change in the weather means a further delay. Rudy is already up and about.

Ablutions in the Antarctic are perfunctory, to say the least. We may be living on top of 70 per cent of the world's fresh water, but it is not easy to get at and unless some thoughtful soul has been up, cut some snow and slipped a block of it into the tank you might as well be in the middle of a desert.

The only washing point is in the kitchen, and shaving into the sink is discouraged. Even in the tent the temperature is only 42 Fahrenheit, so taking clothes off is not comfortable. How on earth anyone has a proper wash in Antarctica I can't imagine, though Patti claims to have managed it.

When I catch sight of myself in the mirror I see disturbingly gaunt features. The cold has tightened my skin. My eyes have sunk and my nose seems to have grown an inch or two. A dark beard-line adds to the impression of a man at the end of his tether, if not at the end of the world.

Make a cup of tea and join Rudy who is deep into an account of Shackleton's expedition to the Antarctic. Shackleton made it to within 97 miles of the Pole, three years before Amundsen.

We still have 600 miles to go. There is no sign of Dan the pilot or anyone else for that matter. The wind rises and falls. Through the window I can see trails of snow scurrying across the ice.

The door is pulled open with difficulty and a round, wrapped bundle is silhouetted against the bright sky before the door slams shut. This bundle stands for a moment, apparently frozen, arms stretched out in front like a penguin, before heaving a deep sigh and beginning to unwrap. Only after several layers of headgear have been shed can you be absolutely sure who has come in.

Scott cooks sourdough pancakes for breakfast. We eat them with 'Lumberjack' syrup. Mike calls the South Pole for a weather check. Visibility is a little hazy, otherwise good. Temperature minus 26 Centigrade. Wind 14 knots. There is no reason for us to stay here. The go-ahead is given to start loading the plane.

Dan, who looks like a plump Lee Marvin, learnt his flying in the USAF and later in Alaska. As we assemble our gear I catch him looking thoughtfully at the plane. I ask him if he knows the Pole well.

He scratches at a white-haired chin: 'Never been there.'

He must enjoy seeing my jaw move up and down, soundlessly, for his eyes have a twinkle as he adds:

'I'm from the north, I've come down south here for the winter . . . to enjoy the nice weather.'

I try to make the best of it, tapping the side of the plane.

'Still, I'll bet this aircraft must have seen plenty of polar action . . .'

'Nope. This'll be the first trip for a single engine turbine Otter to the Pole.'

It transpires that neither pilot nor aircraft, nor even Scott, our Adventure Network escort, has ever been to the Pole. We're all first-timers.

Now I know what Mike Sharp was talking about when he told me yesterday that Adventure Network's success was 'based on enthusiasm . . . really . . . We're an ex-company of adventurers that . . . still want the adventure.'

At 3.45 p.m. we say our farewells, not just to Patriot Hills, but to Basil and Patti, who have to stay behind. Though they have known this all along, it doesn't make it any easier to leave them so close to our final destination.

We squeeze into tiny seats, made smaller by the bulkiness of our clothing. It is rather like sitting at nursery school desks. We share the cabin with a drum of kerosene as well as camera, camping and catering equipment, pumps and ice shovels. The only empty space is the gangway, and that is soon filled with an aluminium ladder.

At 3.50 this tightly-packed collection of people and their props taxis out across the ribbed and rutted ice, turns, and begins the longest and most unconvincing take-off I've ever experienced. It's nothing to do with the pilot, who is completely unconcerned, it's just that the relentless bumping and buffeting of the aeroplane's skis over the sastrugis doesn't seem to be allowing us to gain momentum. The fragmented rock face of the Patriot Hills is approaching fast and my grip tightens on the seat in front. Then with two or three gazelle-like bounces we are airborne, and within seconds the waving group below become specks against the snow.

We are flying into what the locals call 'the interior' – a flat plateau with few distinguishing features, rising from 4000 feet at Patriot Hills to an official 9348 feet at the Pole, though local atmospheric conditions there give a pressure altitude of 10,600 feet.

On the way we have to put down at the Thiel Mountains for a refuelling stop, and to give Dan time to drop some fuel for

Kazama-San's expedition, which will pass nearby.

After two or three approaches as Dan and Scott search for the oil drums, we put down on the ice, at a spot called King's Peak. After two and a half hours sitting in the plane, unable to change position, it is a relief to clamber down onto the ice, even if it is into the teeth of a strong, bitingly cold wind.

Scott puts Rudy and myself to work, assembling a tent. It is, I'm sure, quite simple to those familiar with these matters, but I have never been a happy camper and the cluster of fibreglass rods spells nothing to me but confusion. Scott's patience is wholly commendable.

'They're all colour coded,' he points out, a little tersely. This is no help as my sunglasses distort most colours completely.

After much grunting and groaning and wrestling hopelessly to combine precision assembly with thick polar gloves, we have the tent up and crawl inside to drink tea and coffee and nibble chocolate whilst we wait for Dan to return from dropping Kazama's fuel, some 50 miles away.

Of course, in the dim recesses of one's mind the awareness that we are in sub-zero temperatures 300 miles from the South Pole with no means of transport does cause a flickering of doubt. Not often can one's survival be said to depend on one man, but the prospect of Dan not coming back doesn't really bear thinking about.

The wind-driven snow licks around us. It must be infinitely worse out in the open, away from the protective barrier of King's Peak. All of us are more relieved than we care to show when the scarlet flash of the Otter comes around the mountain again.

Dan takes a last weather check with the Amundsen-Scott Base. As with Russ at the North Pole a great deal of responsibility rests on the pilot at times like this. Dan knows that there is no safe place, no fuel cache at which to land between here and the Pole. It's entirely up to him to evaluate the information and make the final decision. He decides we should go in.

11.30 p.m. We have seen the last of the rock-strewn slopes of the escarpment, now there is nothing but whiteness below in every direction. In front of me Clem settles to sleep. Dan has changed his sealskin hat for a baseball cap, held in place by his headset. Scott is concerned to know if any of us are feeling the effects of altitude – for we are the equivalent of 20,000 feet above sea-level, in an unpressurised plane. I sense that I am taking shorter breaths, but apart from that I feel good, bumped by the excitement of my situation from the tired, almost melancholy heaviness I felt as we sat at King's Peak an hour ago.

DAY 141 · TO THE SOUTH POLE

12.30 a.m. Over the noise of the engine Dan shouts back that we are 47 minutes from the Pole.

1.00 a.m. Radio communication from air traffic control at the South Pole base.

'There is no designated runway and the US Govern-ment cannot authorize you to land. How do you copy?'

Dan: 'OK.'

'OK. Have a good landing.'

Scott gives Rudy a shot of oxygen. The effects of the height can now be clearly felt. Shortage of breath, every movement requiring twice the effort.

1.10 a.m. We can see the South Pole ahead. It is somewhere in the middle of a complex of buildings dominated by a 150-foot wide geodesic dome. Vehicles and building materials are scattered about the site. It is the busiest place we've seen in Antarctica.

1.20 a.m. We land at the Amundsen-Scott South Pole Station, scudding to a halt on a wide, cleared snow runway.

Two well-wrapped figures from the base wait for us to emerge from the plane, and shake our hands in welcome, but the senior of them, an American called Gary, advises us that it is not the policy of the National Science Foundation, who run the base, to offer assistance of a material kind to NGAs – Non-Government Agencies – such as ourselves. Scott confirms that our expedition is self-sufficient and that Adventure Network has a cache of fuel and accommodation located nearby.

Gary, having officially informed us that we are not welcome, brightens up considerably and invites us in for a coffee.

It's as we walk towards the dome, past Portakabins and stacks of wood, insulation equipment, all the flotsam and jetsam of a builders yard, that I become aware of how much effort is required just to keep going. It's as if I'm in a dream. However hard I try the dome doesn't seem to get any nearer.

After what seems like a lifetime we descend between walls carved from the ice to a wide underground entrance, above which a sign informs us that 'The United States of America welcomes you to the Amundsen-Scott South Pole Station.'

No pretence of neutrality here. After travelling 23,000 miles we have found the end of the earth, and it is America.

Pulling open a door as heavy as that on a butcher's deep-freeze we enter a warm, brightly-lit canteen. Music plays. 'If You Leave Me Now', by Chicago. Fresh orange juice and coffee on tap. T-shirts read 'Ski South Pole – 2 miles of base, 12 inches of powder'. A man in Bermuda shorts is piling a tray with chilli dogs, turkey soup, potato chips and lemon poppyseed cake. One of the chefs even *recognizes* me:

'Hey . . . wow! Michael Palin . . . !' He rubs lemon poppyseed cake off on his overalls and proffers a hand.

'Welcome to the Pole!'

The South Pole is on New Zealand Time. Everyone is eating, not because it's 2 o'clock in the morning and they can't sleep, but because we have leapt forward 16 hours, a time-shift of record-breaking proportions. These people are coming in for their evening meal.

Gaze longingly at the hamburgers and French fries, wondering if consumption of either or both would contravene the rules of the National Science Foundation but after a coffee, we trudge back outside. Scott, Fraser, Nigel and Clem go off to dig up the tent which was left here last year, so that we can eat and sleep. Rudy goes back to the plane. I'm about to join them when I realize that in the midst of all these rules, regulations, coffees and poppyseed handshakes I have completely forgotten why we are here.

The temperature, with wind chill, is a cutting, almost paralysing minus 50 Centigrade, and it's 3.15 in the morning at 10,000 feet when I set out on the final lap of this extraordinary journey.

A few hundred yards from the dome, out on the snow, is a semi-circle of flags of all the nations working in Antarctica, in the middle of which is a reflecting globe on a plinth. This is the 'Ceremonial South Pole' at which visiting dignitaries are pictured.

Crunching slowly past it, numb-faced and short of breath, I come at last to a small bronze post sticking three feet above the ground. It looks like an unplumbed lavatory outlet but it exactly marks 90 degrees South. From this spot all directions point north. At this spot I can walk around the world in 8 seconds. At this point with one bound I am back, on 30 degrees East . . . and 30 degrees West, and 72 degrees East and 23 degrees West. I am on the same longitude as Tokyo, Cairo, New York and Sheffield. I am standing at the South Pole.

In the distance I can see a group of anoraked figures pacing the snow, stopping occasionally, forming a circle, pointing then striking at the earth with a shovel. They seem to be repeating this strange ritual over a wide area. Eventually Clem and Nigel and Fraser and Rudy give up looking for the tent and we all stand together at the bottom of the world. Or the top. It depends which way you look at it.

Vocabulary and spelling

1   The following words are taken from the text: 'altitude', 'escarpment', 'ice', 'insulation', 'longitude', 'plateau', 'temperature', 'visibility'. They are concerned with the weather and the geographical conditions at the South Pole. Using a dictionary, find each word and write down a precise definition of its meaning.

2   **Geodesic** means the study of areas of the Earth.

   a) Take the **prefix** 'geo', write it in the middle of your page, and make a spider diagram with as many words as you can think of which begin with the same three letters.

   b) Look up 'geo' in a dictionary. Still looking at the dictionary, add other words that begin in the same way to your spider diagram.

3   These six **polysyllabic** words are from the text: 'irascible', 'perfunctory', 'fragmented', 'commendable', 'melancholy', 'authorize'.

   Using a **Thesaurus**, find and write down three **synonyms** for each word.

4   Take the syllable 'ped' from 'expedition' and find as many words as you can which contain it. The Latin origin for 'ped' is from the family of words connected with foot. For example: **ped**al.

5   Look at the words 'ex**ped**ition' and 'dis**courage**d' from the text. Each word contains another word or **syllable**, which can help you to spell it correctly and to understand its true meaning.

   a) Record these in your Spelling Log

   b) Find six other words in the text which contain familiar words or syllables to help your spelling.

Desolate means neglected or desperate. **Irascible** means bad tempered. **Ablutions** is personal washing. **Perfunctory** means not thorough. **Shackleton** and **Amundsen** are two of the most famous Polar explorers. **Sastrugis** are snow ridges. A **geodesic dome** is a dome for the study of areas of the Earth.

127

Author's craft

1   Re-read the first seven paragraphs of 'Day 140', up to 'Only after several layers of headgear have been shed can you be absolutely sure who has come in.' In this section there are lots of examples of **imagery**.

> **Imagery** is wehre writers use comparisons like similes and metaphors, For example:
> 'Basil…looks like a cross between a bank robber and someone halfway through cosmetic surgery.' This comparison shows how wearing clothing to protect your face in the Antarctic makes you look as you would if you were trying to disguise yourself in a normal climate.

2   Michael Palin's descriptions in both 'Day 140' and 'Day 141' make life at the South Pole seem very uncomfortable. Find as many examples of this as you can.

3 Although it is very different from the other 'Pole to Pole' text, Michael Palin sets out to convey a series of facts about the South Pole, blended with personal experience and opinion. For example:

'we may be living on top of 70 percent of the world's fresh water…', contains a fact that could be rewritten in the **passive voice**: '70 percent of the world's fresh water is found in the ice at the South Pole.'

List four more quotations that contain facts, and rewrite them in the passive voice, in a table like the one below:

Quotation containing a fact	Rewritten in the passive voice
'We may be living on top of 70 percent of the world's fresh water…'	70 percent of the world's fresh water is to be found in the ice at the South Pole

Writing to advise

Michael Palin's 'Pole to Pole' is a mixture of fact, personal experience and opinion. In your reading it is important to be able to tell the difference between **fact** and **opinion**. Above you have already collected some facts from the text.

A **fact** is something that is certain to have happened or to be true. An **opinion** is a point of view, which is short of certain proof.

1 Re-read 'Day 141', and try to find three of Michael Palin's opinions.

2 Imagine that a friend has told you they are going to the South Pole, but they do not know much about what to expect. Base your writing on the experiences outlined in Michael Palin's 'Pole to Pole', and write a letter advising your friend what it is like.

You might include advice on some of the following areas:

- the clothing people wear

- the weather

- what it will feel like at such high altitude

- what there is to see

- what you can do at the South Pole itself

- the buildings there

Think carefully about the style you will use to give advice (your **purpose**) to your friend (your **audience**).

An **audience** for a piece of writing, is the target group of people the text is aimed at.

The **purpose** behind a piece of writing is the reason why it was written. We can write for many purposes. For example: to inform, or to persuade a reader.

3.3 City breaks

Rome

The following text is an advertisement from a travel brochure for a short holiday in Rome, Italy.

The purpose of this text is to persuade the reader to choose Rome rather than any other city for their holiday.

Before you read

Think about what you might need to include in a brochure advertising a place for a short holiday.

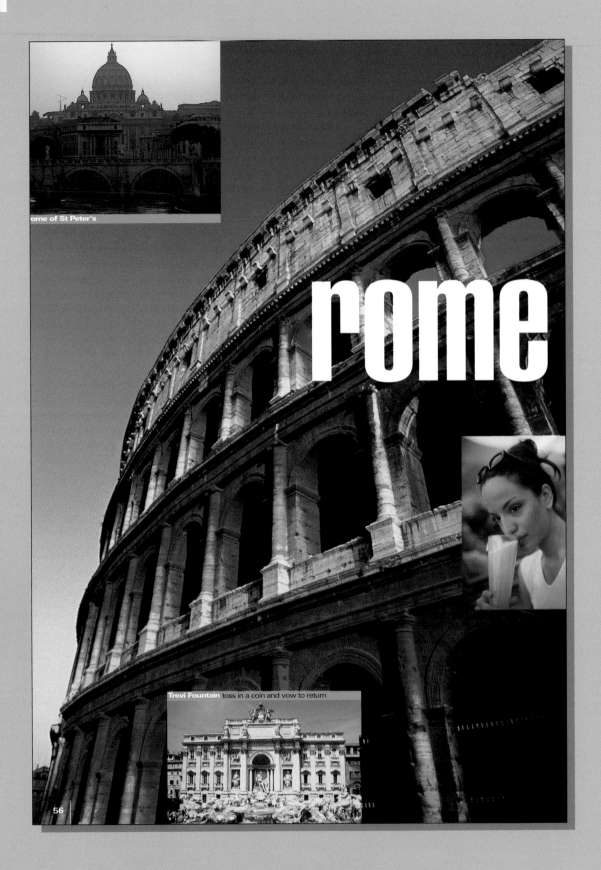

Dome of St Peter's

rome

Trevi Fountain toss in a coin and vow to return

Rome

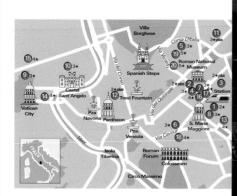

Spanish Steps

Rome has more famous sights than virtually any other city, from the **wonders** of the ancient capital to the artistic and architectural **treasures** of the Renaissance. The Romans live their lives outside and in public, so the city constantly **buzzes** with life. It is noisy, chaotic, vibrant and beautiful…an **unforgettable** experience.

out & about

sightseeing

History and Imperial Rome comes to life in the extensive ruins of the Forum, once the business hub of the Roman Empire, and the massive amphitheatre of the **Colosseum**. Across the Tiber, the magnificent **Dome of St Peter's** dominates Vatican City, home to Michaelangelo's **Sistine Chapel** and countless other masterpieces. Don't miss the **Spanish Steps**, **Pantheon**, **Trevi Fountain** … the list goes on.

shopping

The fine stores of the Via dei Condotti and Via del Corso make for wonderful browsing. Via Nazionale and Via Cola di Rienzo offer a range of shopping, especially for clothes and leather goods, at very reasonable prices.

wining & dining

Nearly all year round the weather permits you to find a pavement or piazza seat outside a café to enjoy a spot of people watching with the locals. There are restaurants and trattorie on every street corner, many offering a tourist menu which often includes wine. **We recommend** Otello near the Spanish Steps - excellent Roman food, or the famous restaurant in the Hotel Massimo D'Azeglio.

special events

Mid-December - 6 January – Christmas Market in the Piazza Navona
19 - 26 July – Festival of folklore of Old Rome, with carnival and fireworks
June – Roman Summer concerts and exhibitions
29 June – St. Peter and St. Paul Patron Saints Day
July – Trinta dei Monti Fashion Show
Late September – Antiques Fair
24 December – Midnight Mass at St. Peter's

public holidays

1, 6 January, 29 March, 1, 25 April, 1 May, 2, 29 June, 15 August, 1 November, 8, 25, 26 December

cost of living

Coffee 60 pence
Beer £2
Meal for two with wine £30
Camera film £4
10 minute taxi ride £6

getting around

A thirty minute train ride from Fiumicino airport brings you to the main station in Rome (approx. £6). The metro can be useful, although its range is limited, while buses and trams have private lanes to help them through the traffic. Within the central area, many sites are within walking distance.

Further information available from the Italian State Tourist Office on 020 7408 1254 or www.romeguide.it

St Peter's Statue

the Vatican Museum

133

Reading for meaning

1 Look at images on the first page of the advertisement on page 132.

a) What do you notice about the camera angle and the colour of the sky in the main image of the Colosseum? Why is it presented like this?

b) What is the purpose of the two insets of the Dome of St Peter's and the Trevi Fountain?

c) What do each of these images show the audience about Rome?

2 Now read the main text on the second page beginning 'Rome has more famous…'

a) Why are there four words printed in bold? What is the intended effect of this selection of vocabulary?

b) Look for examples of persuasive language in the text.

c) How has the writer tried to persuade the reader, or **audience** in each sentence? *Hint: In sentence 1, the writer is appealing to an interest in culture, monuments and buildings.*

d) What is the purpose of the cartoon Roman on the motor scooter? How is this trying to sell Rome?

e) Who is the target audience for this advertisement?

Speaking and listening

1 In groups of four, discuss the similarities and differences between the information text 'Pole to Pole', on pages 114 – 115, and the advertisement from the travel brochure on Rome.

2 Think about:

- the different purposes of each text

- the presentational features, such as headings and sub-headings

- the selection of language

- the layout – composition of images, diagrams and maps.

3 Divide your group into the following roles:

- Student A: the group recorder

- Student B: to lead the discussion on similarities

- Student C: to lead the discussion on differences

- Student D: to present feedback to the class.

Drama

Improvise in pairs.

1 In pairs, improvise a scene at a travel agents. One of you is trying to sell a holiday to the South Pole. The other one can't stand the cold. The travel agent needs to use persuasive language.

2 Change roles. The travel agent is trying to sell a holiday to Rome. Again you will need to use persuasive language, because the customer hates crowds, heat and cultural visits. The customer prefers 'the great outdoors'.

3 Using the following criteria, evaluate your partner's drama work:

a) movement skills – what they did

b) verbal skills – what they said

c) what you liked best about their work

d) what you think could be improved about their work.

Writing to persuade

Using the format for the Rome travel brochure, make a comic advertisement selling a short holiday at the South Pole.

- Use anything you have learned about the South Pole from the two texts you have read.

- Use similar sub-headings to the ones in the Rome advertisement to create your brochure extract.

The natural world

In this section you will read both **fiction** and **non-fiction** texts about some of the least popular living things on the planet. The cane toad and the shark are feared and loathed by many people. Through the reading and writing you do in this section, you will be able to decide for yourself whether these two creatures deserve their reputations.

Research

1   Using a range of sources including textbooks, encyclopaedias and the Internet, research the Australian cane toad, or *bufo marinus*. Collect your information under headings such as: habitat, diet, physical characteristics, behaviour, venom and the history of the toad's spread in Australia.

2   Re-organise the material you have found and make a 'factsheet' called 'The Cane Toad'.

Toad Rage

'Toad Rage' by Morris Gleitzman is the story of a lovable cane toad who is called Limpy, because his leg was run over when he was young. On behalf of all cane toads, especially his little sister Charm, Limpy sets out on a journey to discover why human beings hate cane toads enough to want to swerve across the road in their cars and trucks just to squash them. His cousin Goliath accompanies Limpy on his mission to change the way human beings view the cane toad.

We join the story near the end of Limpy's hilarious journey where, in trying to be chosen as a 'cuddly' mascot for the Olympic Games, he has accidentally passed on a little of his venom to a young Australian pole-vaulter, who has been tested and banned for drug abuse. Limpy decides that he must help her to clear herself.

Toad Rage

Limpy could hear the girl sobbing on her bed as he and Goliath clambered in through the bathroom window and dropped into the bath.

'This is crazy,' muttered Goliath. 'This is gunna end with us having wet cheeks too, except it'll be dog slobber.'

Limpy reached up and put his hands on Goliath's shoulders.

He took a deep breath so his voice wouldn't wobble. This was the most important thing he'd ever said to Goliath, and big cousins sometimes didn't take you seriously if your voice was wobbling.

'Goliath,' said Limpy, 'I want you to stay here.'

Goliath's mouth flopped open.

'I mean it,' said Limpy firmly.

'No way,' said Goliath. 'I'm not letting you go off to be dog meat on your own.'

Limpy took another deep breath. This was exactly what he'd expected Goliath to say.

He looked hard into Goliath's eyes.

'I need you to stay here,' he said. 'Dad will have put the word around by now that I'm on a mission to stop humans killing cane toads. The folks at home don't know I've failed. They don't know they still have to watch out for cars and trucks. It's really important that one of us gets back to warn them.'

Limpy paused while Goliath digested this.

'I'm sure I'll be OK,' he went on, 'but just in case I'm not, you'll have to go back on your own. Get a cockroach to direct you to the city market, find a truck with mangoes painted on the side and stow away.'

Goliath swallowed, and Limpy saw that his cousin's warts were quivering with emotion.

'They're all depending on you Goliath,' he said.

Goliath didn't say anything, and Limpy realised that Goliath was struggling with a voice wobble of his own.

Limpy squeezed Goliath's shoulders, then turned and hopped out of the bath.

He didn't say goodbye.

No point upsetting them both.

The girl was lying face down on the bed, sobbing into her pillow.

Limpy hopped up onto the bedspread and nudged her arm with his shoulder.

She rolled over and opened her eyes.

Limpy hopped round in circles a few times so she'd know it was him and not just any cane toad who happened to be passing.

For a long time she just stared at him, blinking through her tears.

Then her face broke into an amazed grin.

'What are you doing here?'

Limpy could tell she'd recognised him.

Now, he thought, for the tricky bit.

He hopped over and touched her hand with his toenails, careful not to scratch her this time. Then he mimed his own hand hurting, sucking it and blowing on it and waving it around like a truck had just run over it.

He only had to do it for a while before he saw her eyes widen and her mouth fall open and delighted understanding creep across her face.

The Games officials understood immediately.

It took them a while to believe her, though.

Limpy watched as the girl talked animatedly to them and pointed to him and to her hand and mimed a small amount of poison flowing through her blood.

At least, he imagined that's what she was doing. It was pretty hard to see from inside the plastic bag the officials had put him in. The plastic bag had previously had some sort of orange smoked fish in it, and the sides were all smeary and hard to see through.

Limpy rubbed till he had a clear patch.

He watched as the officials kept shaking their heads, right up until the girl grabbed a handful of newspapers and waved them threateningly under their noses.

Then, unhappily, they nodded.

The lab was very bright.

Limpy squinted, partly from the lights and partly from fear.

He knew what could happen to animals in labs.

Please, he begged silently as a man in a white coat put him on a white bench. Please let this human know how to get poison out of a cane toad without any cutting or lethal injections.

Trembling, Limpy wondered if he should help the man.

Squirt at him, just a bit.

He decided not to.

The man put on rubber globes and plastic goggles and squeezed one of Limpy's glands. Pus plopped into a glass bowl.

Limpy felt so weak with relief that he didn't even struggle when the man put him into a glass tank and put a lid on it.

Instead, he watched through the side of the tank as the man did things on the bench with glass tubes and bits of equipment Limpy didn't recognise. Not much lab equipment got chucked out of cars in North Queensland.

The girl and the officials watched too.

Finally, the man in the white coat turned to the girl.

'You're clear,' he said.

Limpy didn't understand at first, not until the girl came grinning over to the tank, took the lid off, and gave him a big kiss.

Later, after Limpy had got over his disappointment about the girl putting the lid back on the tank and leaving without him, he decided it was time to escape.

Later still, after he'd climbed up the wall of the tank about a million times and tried to push the lid off about a million times and fallen on his head about a million times, he realised he couldn't.

Then the lab filled up with humans in white coats, all staring up at a telly on the wall.

On the screen, Limpy saw the girl.

She was in the middle of the stadium, soaring over a crossbar that looked even higher than before.

All the humans in the lab started cheering and hugging each other.

Then they left.

Limpy smiled.

He was glad the girl had made them cheer. She must have done well.

Perhaps she'll come back and kiss me again, thought Limpy hopefully. And then take me back to Goliath.

He waited, not hoping too hard in case she didn't.

A long time passed. Even though he didn't want to, Limpy found himself thinking sadly about Charm.

Then he realised with a start that someone was standing behind the tank, watching him.

It wasn't the girl.

Limpy's insides sank as he saw a clipboard and a red face with hard, shiny eyes.

The bloke in the suit reached into the tank and lifted Limpy out and held him up and stared at him with a thin-lipped expression. Limpy felt pretty sure that whatever was going to happen next wouldn't involve a kiss.

Limpy had never been on a winner's podium at a Games before, and he felt a bit overwhelmed.

It was partly the noise.

A stadium full of humans applauding and cheering was the loudest thing Limpy had ever heard, including some pretty big thunderstorms back home.

Another reason was that he was still in shock.

When the bloke with the clipboard had hurried out of the lab with Limpy in a manila envelope, Limpy had been pretty sure they were heading for somewhere unpleasant.

A loading dock perhaps.

Or a highway so the bloke could run Limpy over in his car.

So when the bloke hurried into the stadium and handed Limpy to the girl just before she stepped onto the podium and received her gold medal, Limpy had been surprised.

The main reason he was a bit overwhelmed, though, was what was happening to him now.

The girl was holding Limpy over her head and the humans in the stadium were cheering even louder.

At him.

Stack me, thought Limpy. I think they like me.

Vocabulary and spelling

In Chapter 26 there are several words containing double **consonants**. For example: 'sobbing', 'slobber', and 'flopping'. It is a common spelling error to write words that need two consonants with only one. In the word word 'sobbing', the vowel 'o' is a short sound. In the word 'sober', the 'o' is a long sound. The double consonant 'bb' shortens the vowel sound.

a) Find and list six words with double consonants.

b) What would each sound like with only one consonant where there should be two?

c) Add these words to your spelling log, and remember to sound the words you write, as you spell them. This will help you to spell these words correctly.

Reading for meaning

1 At the start of Chapter 26, Limpy and Goliath are presented as extremely emotional, in a very human way. What evidence can you find to support this statement?

2 Re-read the section where the girl is trying to prove her innocence, starting: 'The Games officials understood immediately…', at the start of page 139, up to '…the girl came grinning over to the tank, took the lid off, and gave him a big kiss'. Re-write the scene in the laboratory from the girl's point of view. *Hint: Imagine you are the girl, desperate to prove your innocence to the Games officials.*

Media

Imagine that you have been asked to turn 'Toad Rage' into an animated film. As a preview to the film, you have been asked to present Chapter 26 in the form of a **storyboard** containing six **frames**. Write a description of the content of each of your frames underneath your picture.

Writing to inform, explain and describe

- The banning and reinstatement of an athlete, who then goes on to win an Olympic gold medal in the pole vault, would definitely be 'newsworthy'.

- Write a newspaper article telling the story of the athlete's ban, reinstatement, gold medal win, and the cane toad's role. Think carefully about how you need to change the form of the narrative writing in 'Toad Rage', to produce the more formal vocabulary and style required for a newspaper article.

- Begin each paragraph with a **topic** or **lead** sentence. This sentence will refer to the most important things that the rest of the paragraph will go on to explore.

  Here is a paragraph using this pattern which might have appeared in a newspaper before the athlete was reinstated – it begins with a topic sentence.

> 'One of Australia's brightest young female athletes has been disqualified from the Olympic Games after failing a dope test. The popular 19 year old, Janey Jones, had qualified for today's pole-vault final, and was being widely tipped to win a Gold medal, before the shocking news of her ban broke yesterday. Stunned officials delivered the news of Jones' disqualification at a press conference, where it was announced that a blood test had revealed traces of a mysterious prohibited steroid.'

- Select **connectives** and **linking phrases** carefully to ensure that your article develops cohesively from paragraph to paragraph.

Writing to persuade, argue and advise

Using the material you found in your research on cane toads, and anything you have learned from reading the extracts from 'Toad Rage', complete a piece of argumentative writing, entitled 'Should cane toads be eradicated in Australia?' Ensure your own opinion is clear in this writing.

Media texts

> 'Satellites put on the tail of killer sharks' is a newspaper article which explains the dangers of shark attacks off Australian beaches, and which describes the technological system being tried out to track sharks, in order to provide more protection for swimmers. By contrast, 'Just when you thought it was safe' is a newspaper article which presents a balanced attitude towards sharks, and which offers advice about how we can coexist.

Before you read

1 Brainstorm what you know about sharks. Try to list all the different species you know, and include any ideas you might have from the way in which sharks are presented by the media, especially in films.

2 As a class, discuss whether sharks deserve the fearsome reputation they have.

Speaking and listening

1 In groups of four, recount in turn a frightening experience you or someone you know has had with an animal. A shark probably has not attacked you, but you might have been chased by a dog!

2 Include in your account:

   a) a description of the creature, making sure that you make it seem frightening

   b) a clear description of what happened, how the creature moved

   c) how the creature sounded

   d) what the outcome of your experience was.

3 If you have not had such an experience, you may prefer to talk about creatures you are frightened of. For example: spiders or snakes. Explain why you are afraid of them.

4 When everyone has given their account, each group should choose their best to tell the whole class.

Satellites put on the tail of killer sharks

PAUL HAM, SYDNEY

Dangerous waters: five Australian surfers and swimmers have died in a record number of attacks by great white sharks over the past 10 months.

AUSTRALIAN scientists are attaching satellite antennas to the fins of great white sharks – the most feared of the marine predators – to cut down on the growing number of fatal attacks off the country's coast.

Several of the giant fish, immortalised in the film, Jaws, are to be tagged in a programme run

• 25

145

by the Commonwealth Scientific and Industrial Research Organisation (CSIRO), a government institute.

It follows five fatal shark attacks in the past 10 months – far above the previous average of one a year.

Barry Bruce, scientific director of CSIRO, said the satellite link would allow experts to give coastal authorities information that was vital to identifying the beaches most at risk.

"We need to understand how the sharks interact with people."

"If we can establish the sharks' movement patterns, we've got a much better chance of advising swimmers and fishermen of how to avoid them," Bruce said. "We need to understand how the sharks interact with people." The cost of £2,000 a shark is being met by corporate sponsorship. The antennas are designed to be placed in the shark's back at the base of the dorsal fin. Whenever each fish surfaces, – which it does at least once every two days – its precise location will be transmitted to a satellite, which will then beam the information to a CSIRO laboratory in Hobart. A website will track the movements of tagged sharks.

"...double rows of 2-inch serrated teeth"

The warm-blooded, torpedo-shaped shark is one of the most dangerous species to man. With its double rows of 2 in serrated teeth it can grow to 21 ft long and weigh 3,000 kg. It displays a ferocious appetite for anyone who strays across its path while it is pursuing its natural prey of seals, fish and dolphins.

• 26

As you read

Think about whether the article sets out to create a negative image of sharks.

Reading for meaning

1 Write down any words or phrases that present sharks in a dangerous or negative light. For example: 'killer sharks', 'the most feared of marine predators', 'fatal attacks' and 'giant fish' in the first two paragraphs.

2 Read the explanation of how the satellite tracking system works. Write down any words or phrases connected with this technological device. For example: 'scientists are attaching satellite antennas to the fins of great white sharks'. You will need these words and phrases to complete the *Vocabulary* tasks.

Vocabulary

Sharks have roamed the world's oceans for millions of years, and they have fascinated humans for a very long time. But the language used to describe the process of satellite tracking is extremely modern. Even a dictionary twenty years old does not contain the word **website**.

Select five words related to the technology of 'shark tagging', and use a dictionary to find precise definitions for them.

Writing to explain

Using the words and phrases collected in *Reading for meaning* and *Vocabulary*, write a simple three-paragraph explanation for someone who has been asleep for twenty years. This person has no understanding of the technology described in the newspaper article.

You will need to explain the meaning of words like 'satellite' and 'antenna'.

Consider the following paragraph topics:

a) Why the tagging is going ahead

b) Who is tagging the sharks

c) How the sharks are tagged

d) How the sharks are monitored.

Just when you

The potentially most dangerous sharks are considered to be the great white, the tiger shark and the bull shark – but such generalisations can be deceptive: shark behaviour can depend on circumstance as much as species.

Any classic-looking shark (such as silky, dusky, oceanic whitetip, hammerhead or Caribbean reef shark) that is more than 6ft long has got that big by eating its way up the food chain, and can therefore be dangerous. The great hammerhead, which grows to a colossal size, is also worthy of respect. The smaller species usually encountered on coral reefs (such as blacktip, blackfin and whitetip reef sharks) are unlikely to pose a threat.

Shark feeding is, to some extent, a contrived situation, with calculated risks and known rewards (the guarantee that you will be close to sharks): your dive master will tell you how to behave. Encountering sharks in the wild, however, is different.

If you see a shark, stay calm and keep your eyes on it. If it is swimming slowly, it is probably not interested in you and will soon move away.

If the shark is agitated or swimming very quickly, back off as calmly as you can: put some reef between yourself and the shark if possible. If you are with other divers, stay in a close group.

Don't swim or snorkel near deep channels at dawn or dusk, when sharks' feeding activity is at its greatest. Large sharks will tend to enter shallow water

34 •

thought it was safe...

later at night and on a rising tide. Avoid swimming off tropical beaches at night.

Diving and snorkelling is generally safer than swimming or surfing in areas where there are sharks, mostly because you can see what's coming. Irregular splashing on the surface will attract them: many surfers are attacked because their profile on the board resembles a seal or turtle on the surface.

Swimming with marine mammals may be risky – sharks in the vicinity may mistake your splashing for that of an injured mammal.

Avoid areas where people are spear-fishing: sharks are capable of detecting blood in minute quantities from great distances, and will come looking for the source, expecting dinner.

Never provoke sharks, even harmless-seeming nurse sharks, which are often found asleep on the seabed. Divers who think it's fun to pull their tails have, on occasion, discovered that even nurse sharks will bite if molested. ■

• 35

Reading for meaning

Write down any words and phrases that present the shark in a more balanced or positive light than in the previous article. For example: 'The smaller species usually encountered on coral reefs are unlikely to pose a threat', in the second paragraph.

Vocabulary

The writer of 'Just when you thought it was safe…' writes about the 'potential' danger of the shark. Words like 'if', 'can' and 'may' create a **conditional** mood. For example, '*If* it is swimming slowly, it is probably not interested in you.'

1 Find six examples where the writer uses a conditional word to show the potential of sharks when certain conditions apply.

> When we describe writing as **biased**, or as having a particular **bias**, we mean that it sets out to influence the reader to adopt a particular point of view. We could say that the first article is biased, in its negative representation of sharks. The second article, however, offers a more balanced representation of sharks and their potential danger.

2 Using the phrases you collected earlier, make six sentences that demonstrate the contrast in attitudes shown towards sharks in the two articles. Link each of your sentences with a **connective of contrast**, like this model: 'The first article states that the great white shark is "the most feared of the marine predators"', whereas the second article describes the great white as "potentially" one of "the most dangerous sharks"'.

Writing to argue, persuade and advise

The first article says: 'Many locals still insist on swimming in the sea: police were recently forced to chase hundreds of bathers from the waters of Boston Bay, a nearby fishing village, after several big whites were seen in the shallows.'

1 Imagine you are the police chief of Boston Bay. Write a letter to the local newspaper setting out the reasons why it is not safe to bathe there. Add some advice from the second article.

Review

What did you particularly enjoy in this chapter?

What did you not like very much?

Was there anything:

- you found difficult to understand?
- you discovered or understood for the first time?

Use this checklist to help you to answer these questions and review the progress you have made.

You have read: a poem, an extract from a modern novel, a non-fiction information text, an extract from a travel journal, an advertisement and two newspaper articles.

You have thought about how writers use: long and short sentences; made up vocabulary to create humour; pictures and diagrams to inform and persuade; subordinate clauses; bias; poetic techniques; different text types such as poetry, prose, travel writing, advertising and newspaper texts.

You have written: to describe, to compare, to persuade, to advise, to interpret meaning; an advertisement, a factsheet, the storyboard for a film, a narrative, a newspaper article; to argue, to explain, to explore bias; a letter to influence your reader.

To improve your writing, you have thought about: planning with grids, spider diagrams and writing frames; selecting vocabulary and the effect of new technology on language; verbs and tenses; using quotations, organising paragraphs, commas and semi-colons; fact and opinion, spelling; the conventions of different genres; connectives of contrast; media techniques and subordinate clauses.

Your speaking and listening work has included: brainstorming in pairs, whole class discussion, making tableaux, collaborative reading aloud, improvising in pairs, discussing in groups, role playing, peer evaluation of drama, recounting a story.

You may have used ICT: to research on the Internet; to write a factsheet; to draft and redraft and to set out your work in the form of a travel brochure, and a newspaper article; to use a spellcheck.

④ Humour

In this chapter you will read poems, stories and plays that have been written to make us smile or laugh. Writers use different techniques to add humour to their work and you will learn about these and have opportunities to practise them yourself.

A writer might decide to use humour for a number of reasons; it could be that she wants to entertain the reader. But humour is also used for more serious purposes. Sometimes comedy is used when we want to make people question the normal order of things and make them see things in a different way.

4.1 Is this love?

Bridget Jones's Diary

This extract is taken from the novel 'Bridget Jones's Diary' by Helen Fielding. Bridget, the character writing the diary, is a single woman in her early thirties. The diary charts the ups and downs of one year in Bridget's life and her obsessions with chocolate, smoking and romance.

Before you read

1   What diaries have you read or heard of? Which of the diaries that you have come across are real and which are fictional?

2   Why do you think people write diaries?

3   What details do you think Bridget's diary will include and in what style might she write?

Monday 13 February

9st 1, alcohol units 5, cigarettes 0 (spiritual enrichment removes need to smoke – massive breakthrough), calories 2845.

Though heartbroken by my parents' distress, I have to admit parallel and shameful feeling of smugness over my new role as carer and, though I say it myself, wise counsellor. It is so long since I have done anything at all for anyone else that it is a totally new and heady sensation. This is what has been missing in my life. I am having fantasies about becoming a Samaritan or Sunday school teacher, making soup for the homeless (or, as my friend Tom suggested, darling mini bruschettas with pesto sauce), or even retraining as a doctor. Maybe going out with a doctor would be better still, both sexually and spiritually fulfilling. I even began to wonder about putting an ad in the lonely hearts column of the *Lancet*. I could take his messages, tell patients wanting night visits to bugger off, cook him

---

little goats-cheese soufflés, then end up in a foul mood with him when I am sixty, like Mum.

Oh God. Valentine's Day tomorrow. Why? Why? Why is entire world geared to make people not involved in romance feel stupid when everyone knows romance does not work anyway. Look at royal family. Look at Mum and Dad.

Valentine's Day purely commercial, cynical enterprise, anyway. Matter of supreme indifference to me.

Tuesday 14 February

9st, alcohol units 2 (romantic Valentine's Day treat – 2 bottles Becks, on own, huh), cigarettes 12, calories 1545.

8 a.m. Oooh, goody. Valentine's Day. Wonder if the post has come yet. Maybe there will be a card from Daniel. Or a secret admirer. Or some flowers or heart-shaped chocolates. Quite excited, actually.

Brief moment of wild joy when discovered bunch of roses in the hallway. Daniel! Rushed down and gleefully picked them up just as the downstairs-flat door opened and Vanessa came out.

'Ooh, they look nice,' she said enviously. 'Who are they from?'

'I don't know!' I said coyly, glancing down at the card. 'Ah . . .' I tailed off. 'They're for you.'

'Never mind. Look this is for you,' said Vanessa, encouragingly. It was an Access bill.

Decided to have cappuccino and chocolate croissants on way to work to cheer self up. Do not care about figure. Is no point as no one loves or cares about me.

On the way in on the tube you could see who had had Valentine cards and who hadn't. Everyone was looking round trying to catch each other's eye and either smirking or looking away defensively.

Got into the office to find Perpetua had a bunch of flowers the size of a sheep on her desk.

'Well, Bridget,' she bellowed so that everyone could hear. 'How many did you get?'

I slumped into my seat muttering, 'Shudurrrrrrrp,' out of the side of my mouth like a humiliated teenager.

'Come on. How many?'

I thought she was going to get hold of my earlobe and start twisting it or something.

'The whole thing is ridiculous and meaningless. Complete commercial exploitation.'

'I knew you didn't get any,' crowed Perpetua. It was only then that I noticed Daniel was listening to us across the room and laughing.

Wednesday 15 February

Unexpected surprise. Was just leaving flat for work when noticed there was a pink envelope on the table – obviously a late Valentine – which said, 'To the Dusky Beauty'. For a moment I was excited, imagining it was for me and suddenly seeing myself as a dark mysterious object of desire to men out in the street. Then I remembered bloody Vanessa and her slinky dark bob. Humph.

9 p.m. Just got back and card is still there.

10 p.m. Still there.

11 p.m. Unbelievable. The card is still there. Maybe Vanessa hasn't got back yet.

Thursday 16 February

8st 12 (weight loss through use of stairs), alcohol units 0 (excellent), cigarettes 5 (excellent), calories 2452 (not v.g.), times gone down stairs to check for Valentine-type envelope 18 (bad psychologically but v.g. exercise-wise).

The card is still there! Obviously it is like eating the last Milk Tray or taking the last slice of cake. We are both too polite to take it.

Friday 17 February

8st 12, alcohol units I (v.g.), cigarettes 2 (v.g), calories 3241 (bad but burnt off by stairs), checks on card 12 (obsessive).

9 a.m. Card is still there.

9 p.m. Still there.

9.30 p.m. Still there. Could stand it no longer. Could tell Vanessa was in as cooking smells emanating from flat, so knocked on door. 'I think this must be for you,' I said, holding out the card as she opened the door.

'Oh, I thought it must be for you,' she said.

'Shall we open it?' I said.

'OK'. I handed it to her, she gave it back to me, giggling. I gave it back to her. I love girls.

'Go on,' I said, and she slit open the envelope with the kitchen knife she was holding. It was rather an arty card – as if it might have been bought in an art gallery.

She pulled a face.

'Means nothing to me,' she said, holding out the card.

Inside it said, 'A piece of ridiculous and meaningless commercial exploitation – for my darling little frigid cow.'

I let out a high-pitched noise.

10 p.m. Just called Sharon and recounted whole thing to her. She said I should not allow my head to be turned by a cheap card and should lay off Daniel as he is not a very nice person and no good will come of it.

Called Tom for second opinion, particularly on whether I should call Daniel over the weekend. 'Nooooooooo!' he yelled. He asked me various probing questions: for example, what Daniel's behaviour had been like over the last few days when, having sent the card, he had had no response from me. I reported that he had seemed flirtier than usual. Tom's prescription was wait till next week and remain aloof.

Reading for meaning

1   How is Bridget feeling on Monday 13 February?

2   How does Fielding build up a sense of anticipation in the Tuesday 14 February diary entry? *Hint: You should consider length of sentence at the start of the entry, repetition, choice of adjectives and adverbs in the first 9 lines.*

An **adverb** often adds to the meaning of a **verb** by giving detail about the way in which someone speaks, acts or thinks. They can give clues as to a person's mood. Think about how the adverbs in the examples below change what you learn about the woman.

• The woman spoke **harshly** to the boy.
• The woman spoke **hurriedly** to the boy.

3 Chart a timeline of Bridget's emotions over the Valentine's Day period. What impression do you get of Bridget's character?

4 Look at the end of Monday 13 February and the start of Tuesday 14 February. In what way do they seem to contradict one another? What effect is Fielding trying to establish?

5 Find three different examples of humour in this extract. Try to explain what makes each example funny.

Vocabulary, style and language variation

1 Why does Fielding put a section in *italics* at the start of each entry to the diary?

2 Why do you think Fielding wrote this novel in diary form? Consider:

- how Fielding creates a sense of Bridget's voice through word choice and use of **colloquial language**

- the use of **note form** and explanation

- how changes in time are revealed to the reader.

Note form can be used to create a sense of informality, intimacy or rush. Typically sentences will be incomplete. For example: 'Gone out.' Informal punctuation, such as dashes, will be used.

Writing to imagine, explore and entertain

1 Who do you think sent Bridget the Valentine? Think about the motivations for Tom, Perpetua and Sharon. Decide who you think sent the card. Write their diary entry for the day describing why they sent it and the impact they hope it will have on Bridget.

2 Write Bridget's diary entry for Saturday 18 February. Does she follow her friends' advice?

You should aim to imitate Fielding's style. Use a combination of short and long sentences to create a sense of informality and immediacy. Also consider your use of punctuation and choice of vocabulary to reflect Bridget's character and add intimacy to the entry.

Writing to persuade and to argue

Imagine you have been asked to write an article for a magazine for people of your age exploring the tradition of Valentine's Day.

1   First you must decide which of the viewpoints given below you are going to assume for the focus of your article:

- Valentine's Day is a purely commercial enterprise

- Valentine's Day is innocent fun.

2   Research the tradition of Valentine's Day to help introduce your article. Try to include some of the techniques of argumentative writing listed below:

- confident and assertive tone explaining your point of view

- controlled use of humour and use of the pronoun to put forward a serious point in an engaging way

- use of the pronoun 'you' to make your reader feel as if the article is speaking to them directly

- use of **rhetorical questions**.

Drama

1   In pairs, improvise a telephone conversation between Bridget and her mum where Bridget explains her Valentine's Day experience.

- Would Bridget tell her mum the full story?

- Would her mum listen carefully and offer advice or would she be too caught up with her own concerns about herself and Bridget's dad?

2   Now, imagine you are Perpetua and Sharon in Bridget's office on the day she tells everyone she has received a Valentine. Devise the conversation that Perpetua and Sharon might have as they speculate who sent the Valentine. Look back at the extract to check the relationship Bridget has with the other women in her office.

Shakespeare – Twelfth Night

Here you will be studying a series of extracts taken from 'Twelfth Night' by William Shakespeare. In these extracts you will focus upon Malvolio looking at his character and his relationships with others in the play.

The play is set in an imaginary country called Illyria. Much of the action takes place in the Countess Olivia's house where Sir Andrew Aguecheek is staying with Sir Toby Belch, who believes he is in love with Olivia. Malvolio is Olivia's rather arrogant head servant. Maria is Olivia's maid.

As the scene starts, Malvolio has just left the stage, having told off Sir Toby, Olivia's uncle, and Sir Andrew Aguecheek, his friend for making a drunken noise that might disturb Olivia. It is night time and she is trying to sleep. Toby, Andrew and Maria are annoyed with him and decide to get their own back.

Before you read

1 Using the internet, find out what and when Twelfth Night is and prepare a brief summary for the class.

2 Look at the names of the characters. What would you expect each of them to be like? Be prepared to explain what it is about the name that suggests those characteristics to you.

Twelfth Night

MARIA   The devil a puritan that he (Malvolio) is, or anything
constantly but a time-pleaser, an affectioned ass, that cons   125
state without book and utters it by great swarths. The best
persuaded of himself: so crammed (as he thinks) with
excellencies, that it is his grounds of faith that all that look on
him love him; and on that vice in him will my revenge find
notable cause to work.   130

SIR TOBY   What wilt thou do?

MARIA   I will drop in his way some obscure epistles of love,
wherein by the colour of his beard, the shape of his leg,
the manner of his gait, the expressure of his eye, forehead,
and complexion, he shall find himself most feelingly   135
personated. I can write very like my lady your niece; on a
forgotten matter we can hardly make distinction of our hands.

SIR TOBY   Excellent, I smell a device.

SIR ANDREW   I have't in my nose, too.

SIR TOBY   He shall think by the letters that thou wilt drop that   140
they come from my niece, and that she's in love with him.

MARIA   My purpose is indeed a horse of that colour.

SIR ANDREW   And your horse now would make him an ass.

MARIA   Ass, I doubt not.

Reading for meaning

1   Look closely at Maria's description of Malvolio once he has left.
What do you think she means by the following phrases:
'time-pleaser', 'an affectioned ass', 'the best persuaded of himself',
'crammed with excellencies'?

2   Using the information in your answer to excercise 1 write a brief
character sketch of Malvolio using two or three quotations to
support your points about him.

3   a) What plan does Maria have in mind?

b) Why do you think she is keen to play a trick on Malvolio?

This next scene takes place in Olivia's garden. Maria has forged a letter in Olivia's handwriting to trick Malvolio into believing that Olivia is in love with him. She has left the letter in Malvolio's path and has hidden herself with Sir Toby, Sir Andrew and another man, Fabian, to watch what happens.

MALVOLIO   [Taking up the letter] What employment have we here?

SIR TOBY   Now is the woodcock near the gin.

FABIAN   O peace, and the spirit of humours intimate reading aloud   70
to him!

MALVOLIO   By my life, this is my lady's hand: these be her very c's,
her u's, and her t's, and thus makes she her great P's. It is, in
contempt of question, her hand.

SIR ANDREW   Her c's, her u's, and her t's: why that?   75

MALVOLIO [Reads]   'To the unknown beloved, this, and my good
wishes' – her very phrases! By your leave, wax. Soft! And the
impressure her Lucrece, with which she uses to seal: 'tis my
lady. To whom should this be? [Opens the letter]

FABIAN   This wins him, liver and all.   80

MALVOLIO [Reads]   *Jove knows I love,*
but who?
Lips, do not move:
No man must know.
'*No man must know.*' What follows? The numbers altered!   85
'*No man must know*'! If this should be thee, Malvolio?

SIR TOBY   Marry, hang thee, brock!

MALVOLIO [Reads]   *I may command where I adore,*
But silence, like a Lucrece knife,
With bloodless stroke my heart doth gore;   90
M.O.A.I. doth sway my life.

FABIAN   A fustian riddle!

> SIR TOBY   Excellent wench, say I.
>
> MALVOLIO   '*M.O.A.I. doth sway my life.*' Nay, but first let me
> see, let me see, let me see.   95
>
> FABIAN   What dish o' poison has she dressed him!
>
> SIR TOBY   And with what wing the staniel checks at it!

Drama

In groups of five prepare a performance of this scene. Remember to bear in mind what makes this scene funny.

- Modern directors have to decide whether to cut any of the lines to make the action and language appropriate for their audience. Re-read the scene in your group and decide if you are going to edit the lines you will deliver.

- Now think about the positions of each character over the course of the episode. How can the staging add to the humour for your audience? Sketch out a plan of positions.

- Focus upon the character Malvolio. In your group consider how an actor could use voice, (volume, emphasis, pause), body language, facial expression and movement around the stage to put across Malvolio's character and amuse the audience.

- Next consider what the tricksters might be doing as Malvolio reads the letter aloud. Do you think they would mimic Malvolio?

- How will you conclude? What pose will the tricksters strike? How might Malvolio exit?

- In your group decide who will take each part and prepare your scene.

In this final extract Malvolio meets Olivia ready to woo her. He has acted upon some of the suggestions in the letter.

MALVOLIO '*I may command where I adore.*' Why, she may
command me: I serve her; she is my lady. Why, this is evident
to any formal capacity. There is no obstruction in this, and the   100
end - what should that alphabetical position portend? If I
could make that resemble something in me – Softly! '*M.O.A.I.*'

SIR TOBY   O ay, make up that! He is now at a cold scent.

FABIAN   Sowter will cry upon't for all this, though it be as rank
as a fox.   105

MALVOLIO   'M'– Malvolio. 'M' – why, that begins my name!

FABIAN   Did not I say he would work it out? The cur is excellent
at faults.

MALVOLIO   'M' – but then there is no consonancy in the sequel that
suffers under probation. 'A' should follow, but 'O' does.   110

FABIAN   And O shall end, I hope.

SIR TOBY   Ay, or I'll cudgel him and make him cry 'O'!

MALVOLIO   And then 'I' comes behind.

FABIAN   Ay, and you had any eye behind you, you might see
more detraction at your heels than fortunes before you.   115

MALVOLIO   '*M.O.A.I.*' This simulation is not as the former, and
yet, to crush this a little, it would bow to me, for every one
of these letters are in my name. Soft, here follows prose.
[Reads] '*If this fall into thy hand, revolve. In my stars I am
above thee, but be not afraid of greatness. Some are born*   120
great, some achieve greatness, and some have greatness
thrust upon them. Thy fates open their hands; let thy blood
and spirit embrace them, and, to inure thyself to what thou
art like to be, cast thy humble slough and appear fresh. Be

opposite with a kinsman, surly with servants; let thy tongue 125
tang arguments of state; put thyself into the trick of
singularity. She thus advises thee that sighs for thee.
Remember who commended thy yellow stockings and
wished to see thee ever cross-gartered: I say, remember.
Go to, thou art made if thou desir'st to be so; if not, let me 130
see thee a steward still, the fellow of servants, and not
worthy to touch Fortune's fingers. Farewell. She that
would alter services with thee,

The Fortunate-Unhappy.'

Daylight and champain discovers not more! This is open. 135
I will be proud, I will read politic authors, I will baffle Sir Toby,
I will wash off gross acquaintance, I will be point-device, the
very man. I do not now fool myself to let imagination jade me;
for every reason excites to this, that my lady loves me. She did
commend my yellow stockings of late, she did praise my leg 140
being cross-gartered; and in this she manifests herself to my
love, and with a kind of injunction drives me to these habits
of her liking. I thank my stars, I am happy. I will be strange,
stout, in yellow stockings, and cross-gartered, even with the
swiftness of putting on. Jove and my stars be praised! Here is 145
yet a postscript. [Reads] 'Thou canst not choose but know
who I am. If thou entertain'st my love, let it appear in thy
smiling; thy smiles become thee well. Therefore in my
presence still smile, dear my sweet, I prithee.' Jove, I thank
thee. I will smile; I will do every thing that thou wilt have me. 150
[Exit]

Enter [MARIA with] Malvolio

OLIVIA   How now, Malvolio?

MALVOLIO   Sweet lady, ho, ho!

OLIVIA   Smil'st thou? I sent for thee upon a sad occasion.

MALVOLIO   Sad, lady? I could be sad. This does make some
    obstruction in the blood, this cross-gartering, but what of that? 20
    If it please the eye of one, it is with me as the very true
    sonnet is: 'Please one, and please all.'

OLIVIA   Why, how dost thou, man? What is the matter with thee?

MALVOLIO   Not black in my mind, though yellow in my legs.
It did come to his hands, and commands shall be executed.   25
I think we do know the sweet Roman hand.

OLIVIA   Wilt thou go to bed, Malvolio?

MALVOLIO   To bed? Ay, sweetheart, and I'll come to thee.

OLIVIA   God comfort thee! Why dost thou smile so and kiss
thy hand so oft.   30

MARIA   How do you, Malvolio?

MALVOLIO   At your request! Yes, nightingales answer daws!

MARIA   Why appear you with this ridiculous boldness before
my lady?

MALVOLIO   '*Be not afraid of greatness*': 'twas well writ.   35

OLIVIA   What mean'st thou by that, Malvolio?

MALVOLIO   '*Some are born great –*'

OLIVIA   Ha?

MALVOLIO   '*Some achieve greatness –*'

OLIVIA   What say'st thou?   40

MALVOLIO   '*And some have greatness thrust upon them.*'

OLIVIA   Heaven restore thee!

MALVOLIO   '*Remember who commended thy yellow stockings –*'

OLIVIA   Thy yellow stockings?

MALVOLIO   '*And wished to see thee cross-gartered.*'   45

OLIVIA   Cross-gartered?

MALVOLIO   '*Go to, thou art made, if thou desir'st to be so –*'

OLIVIA   Am I made?

MALVOLIO   '*If not, let me see thee a servant still.*'

OLIVIA   Why, this is very midsummer madness. Good Maria,   50
let this fellow be looked to. Where's my cousin Toby? Let
some of my people have a special care of him; I would not
have him miscarry for the half of my dowry.

[Exeunt OLIVIA and MARIA]

165

Reading for meaning

Think about Malvolio's tormentors. Does Malvolio get what he deserves?

Writing to inform, explain and describe

1   Imagine you have been elected to be 'Lord of Misrule' for one day in your school. Think back to your research on the festival 'Twelfth Night'. Describe the day making sure that you show the humour of a topsy-turvy world. Make sure that order wins in the end.

Think about:

● using adjectives to create the scene, allowing your reader to visualise it

● including a variety of sentence lengths to hold the readers' attention at key moments

● which aspects of school life would offer most humour if turned upside down.

2   Imagine you are Maria. Write a letter to a friend at the end of each of these extracts explaining your thoughts and feelings about the events as they unfold and your responses to the other characters.

You should consider:

● her reasons for tricking Malvolio and her attitude towards him at the start

● the way she manages to include others in the trick and her thoughts about the three men as they watch Malvolio

● Malvolio's response to her letter

You might want to write your letter using a letter template in a word processing programme on a computer. Choose a font to suit Maria, and check your spelling with the spellchecker.

The Miller's Tale

Geoffrey Chaucer is probably the most well-known English medieval writer and poet. He worked as a courtier, civil servant and sometimes as a diplomat for the king. His famous 'Canterbury Tales' are told by a group of people as they travel on a five-day journey to Canterbury as a way to keep the other travellers entertained. The characters that tell the stories come from a wide range of backgrounds and occupations. This extract is taken from 'The Miller's Tale'. The miller is big boned and red-headed with flaring nostrils and a skull so thick he could head-butt a door and break it open! As he walks along, he plays the bagpipes and tells his story of a young wife, Alison, and her two lovers, Nicholas and Absalon. In this section Absalon gets up early to visit Alison, who is in bed with Nicholas.

 ### Before you read

1 Discuss with a partner the things that make you laugh. Do you think that what we laugh at has changed over time?

2 Research **slapstick** humour. What does this phrase mean? Your teacher might provide you with examples from famous comedy duos such as Laurel and Hardy or Morecambe and Wise.

The Miller's Tale   (Middle English)

Section one

When that the firste cok hath crowe, anon
Up rist this joly lovere Absolon,
And hym arraieth gay, at poynt-devys.
But first he cheweth greyn and lycorys,
To smellen sweete, er he hadde kembd his heer,
Under his tonge a trewe-love he beer,
For thereby wende he to ben gracious.
He rometh to the carpenteres hous,
And stille he stant under the shot-wyndowe –
Unto his brest it raughte, it was so lowe – 10
And softe he cougheth with a semy soun:
"What do ye, hony-comb, sweete Alisoun,
My faire bryd, my sweete cynamome?
Awaketh, lemman myn, and speketh to me!
Wel litel thynken ye upon my wo,
That for youre love I swete ther I go,
No wonder is thogh that I swelte and swete;
I moorne as dooth a lamb after the tete.
Ywis, lemman, I have swich love-longynge,
That lik a turtel trewe is my moornynge. 20
I may nat ete na moore than a mayde."
"Go fro the wyndow, Jakke fool," she sayde;
"As help me God, it wol nat be 'com pa me.'
I leve another – and elles I were to blame –
Wel bet than thee, by Jhesu, Absolon.
Go forth thy wey, or I wol caste a ston,
And lat me slepe, a twenty devel wey!"
 "Alas," quod Absolon "and weylawey,
That trewe love was evere so yvel biset!
Thanne kysse me; syn it may be no bet, 30
For Jhesus love, and for the love of me."
"Wiltow thanne go thy wey therwith?" quod she.
"Ye, certes, lemman," quod this Absolon.
"Thanne make thee redy," quod she, "I come anon."
And unto Nicholas she seyde stille,
"Now hust, and thou shalt laughen al thy fille."

The Miller's Tale (Modern version by Neville Coghill)

Section one

The first cock crew at last, and thereupon
Up rose this jolly lover Absalon
In gayest clothes, garnished with that and this;
But first he chewed a grain of liquorice
To charm his breath before he combed his hair.
Under his tongue the comfit nestling there
Would make him gracious. He began to roam
Towards the carpenter's; he reached their home
And by the casement window took his stand.
Breast-high it stood, no higher than his hand.
He gave a cough, it was a semi-sound;
'Alison, honey-comb, are you around?
Sweet cinnamon, my little pretty bird,
Sweetheart, wake up and say a little word!
You seldom think of me in all my woe,
I sweat for love of you wherever I go!
No wonder if I do, I pine and bleat
As any lambkin hungering for the teat.
Believe me, darling, I'm so deep in love
I croon with longing like a turtle-dove,
I eat as little as a girl at school.'
'You go away,' she answered, 'you Tom-fool!
There's no come-up-and-kiss-me here for you.
I love another and why shouldn't I too?
Better than you, by Jesu, Absalon!
Take yourself off or I shall throw a stone.
I want to get some sleep. You go to Hell!'
'Alas,' said Absalon. 'I knew it well;
True love is always mocked and girded at;
So kiss me, if you can't do more than that,
For Jesu's love and for the love of me!'
'And if I do, will you be off?' said she.
'Promise you, darling,' answered Absalon.
'Get ready then; wait, I'll put something on,'
She said and then she added under breath
To Nicholas, 'Hush . . . we shall laugh to death!'

Section two (Middle English)
This Absolon doun sette hym on his knees
And seyde, "I am a lord at alle degrees;
For after this I hope ther cometh moore.
Lemman, thy grace, and sweete bryd, thyn oore!"   40
 The wyndow she undoth, and that in haste.
"Have do," quod she, "com of, and speed the faste,
Lest that oure neighebores thee espie."
 This Absolon gan wype his mouth ful drie,
Derk was the nyght as pich, or as the cole,
And at the wyndow out she putte hir hole,
And Absolon, hym fil no bet ne wers,
But with his mouth he kiste hir naked ers
Ful savourly, er he were war of this.
Abak he stirte, and thoughte it was amys,   50
For wel he wiste a womman hath no berd.
He felte a thyng al rough and long yherd,
And seyde, "Fy! allas! what have I do?"
"Tehee!" quod she, and clapte the wyndow to,
And Absolon gooth forth a sory pas.
"A berd! a berd!" quod hende Nicholas,
"By Goddes corpus, this goth faire and weel.
This sely Absolon herde every deel,
And on his lippe he gan for anger byte,
And to hymself he seyde. "I shal thee quyte."

Section two (Modern version)
This Absalon went down upon his knees;
'I am a lord!' he thought, 'And by degrees
There may be more to come; the plot may thicken.'
'Mercy, my love,' he said, 'Your mouth, my chicken!'
 She flung the window open then in haste
And said, 'Have done, come on, no time to waste,
The neighbours here are always on the spy.
 Absalon started wiping his mouth dry.

Dark was the night as pitch, as black as coal,
And at the window out she put her hole,
And Absalon, so fortune framed the farce,
Put up his mouth and kissed her naked arse
Most savorously before he knew of this.
 And back he started. Something was amiss;
He knew quite well a woman has no beard,
Yet something rough and hairy had appeared.
'What have I done?' he said. 'Can that be you?'
'Teehee!' she cried and clapped the window to.
Off went poor Absalon sadly through the dark.
'A beard! a beard!' cried Nicholas the Spark.
'God's body, that was something like a joke!'
And Absalon, overhearing what he spoke,
Bit on his lips and nearly threw a fit
In rage and thought, 'I'll pay you back for it!'

Section three (Middle English)
He cogheth first and knokketh therwithal   60
Upon the wyndowe, right as he dide er,
 This Alison answerde, "Who is ther
That knokketh so? I warrante it a theef."
 "Why nay," quod he, "God woot, my sweete leef,
I am thyn Absolon, my deerelyng.
Of gold," quod he, "I have thee broght a ryng.
My mooder yaf it me, so God me save;
Ful fyn it is, and therto wel ygrave.
This wol I yeve thee, if thou me kisse."
 This Nicholas was risen for to pisse,   70
And thoughte he wolde amenden al the jape;
He sholde kisse his ers er that he scape.
And up the wyndowe dide he hastily,
And out his ers he putteth pryvely
Over the buttok to the haunche-bon;
And therwith spak this clerk, this Absolon,
"Spek, sweete bryd, I noot nat where thou art."
 This Nicholas anon leet fle a fart,
As greet as it had been a thonder-dent,
That with the strook he was almoost yblent;   80
And he was redy with his iren hoot,
And Nicholas amydde the ers he smoot.

Section three (Modern version)

...   He knocked and gave a little call
Under the window as he had before.
Alison said, 'There's someone at the door.
Who's knocking there? I'll warrant it's a thief.'
'Why, no,' said he, 'my little flower-leaf,
It's your own Absalon, my sweety-thing!
Look what I've brought you – it's a golden ring
My mother gave me, as I may be saved.
It's very fine, and prettily engraved;
I'll give it to you, darling, for a kiss.'
 Now Nicholas had risen for a piss,
And thought he could improve upon the jape
And make him kiss his arse ere he escape,
And opening the window with a jerk,
Stuck out his arse, a handsome piece of work,
Buttocks and all, as far as to the haunch.
 Said Absalon, all set to make a launch,
'Speak, pretty bird, I know not where thou art!'
This Nicholas at once let fly a fart
As loud as if it were a thunder-clap.
He was near blinded by the blast, poor chap,
But his hot iron was ready; with a thump
He smote him in the middle of the rump.

Reading for meaning

Read the first section.

1 a) What preparation does Absalon make before setting out?

   b) What does this tell you about him?

2 What does Absalon say to Alison in his opening speech to try to persuade her that he cares for her? *Hint: Think about the words he uses to describe her and the imagery he employs.*

3 a) Look at Alison's reply. What do you infer about her from her words?

   b) At what point did you realise Alison intended to play a trick on Absalon? Quote the line and explain it.

4 a) Describe the trick Alison plays.

   b) How did you react to this when you read it?

Read the second section.

Absalon has vowed to get his revenge. He visits the blacksmith who lends him a red-hot poker. He then quickly returns to Alison's house.

1 What does Absalon say to persuade Alison to come to the window again?

2 a) Describe what happens when Nicholas comes to the window.

   b) Do you feel any sympathy for any of these characters? Why? Why not?

Chaucer's technique

The tales were designed to be read aloud to an audience to listen to, rather than to be read by an individual reader.

1   Discuss in pairs how Chaucer's use of **rhythm** and **rhyme** could help to make the poem more accessible to a listener. *Hint: It might help to remember that rhythm relies on beats in a line and rhyme relies on sound.*

2   In the extract the word 'well' rhymes with 'Hell' on the previous line, even though it refers to Absalon's knowledge of love. Why do you think Chaucer has done this? *Hint: Look at the glossary to help you.*

3   Another sound effect used by Chaucer is **alliteration**.

   a) Look at the fifth line of the original text. Identify the alliteration.

   b) Skim the original looking for the frequency of this technique. It was popular at the time Chaucer was working. Are you surprised at the extent of alliteration?

   c) Why do you think Chaucer used this literary device? *Hint: Refer to Chapter One to remind you what alliteration means.*

The term **rhyming couplet** describes two consecutive lines of a poem that are united by the fact that they rhyme. It is worthwhile noting that in using rhyme a poet creates echoes between words that can adjust or emphasise meaning, perhaps even creating a link between the words that adds further meaning to the verse. For example: consider how the words 'room' and 'tomb' work together.

Language change

You have been given two versions of this extract. One is written in Middle English and the second provides a modern 'translation'. There are not many words that have become obsolete, but sometimes the meaning or spelling of Chaucer's words has changed over time.

Look at the words in the box below. Complete the chart to show the modern equivalent and then suggest what has changed over time.

Chaucer		Modern English
Hath	(line 1)	
Cheweth	(line 4)	
Rometh	(line 8)	
Wyndowe	(line 9)	
Thyn	(line 40)	
Cogheth	(line 60)	
Knokketh	(line 60)	
Deerelyng	(line 65)	
Ryng	(line 66)	
Fyn	(line 68)	

Writing to imagine, explore and entertain

Chaucer's tale has many twists to ensure the listener is kept interested and amused. He also uses **slapstick** humour to appeal to his audience.

Write a short, amusing story with a twist at the end of the tale. Before you begin writing, consider if you want the twist to be connected to a character or an event and how you will guide your reader to expect one thing and then deliver another.

Drama

Although looking at the original Middle English text might seem daunting, provided you follow a few ground rules reading Chaucer out loud can be quite good fun.

Spelling was not yet standardised in the fourteenth century, so Chaucer could change this depending on the length of line or rhyme he wanted but pronunciation would stay the same.

To read Chaucer out loud, remember that consonants were all pronounced, including letters which have now become silent such as the 'l' in 'calf' or 'folk' or the 'k' in 'knight'. The letter 'e' on the end of a word was spoken if the next word began with a consonant.

1 Practise speaking the lines Absalon says on his return 'Why nay,' to 'if thou me kisse.' Your teacher might make other suggestions. Share your delivery with the rest of the class.

2 Do you find it easier to understand the spoken or the written version of Chaucer's tale? Why do you think that this might be?

Poems by John Hegley

These poems are taken from the work of the poet John Hegley. His work is a mixture of cartoon, poetry, observation and comedy. He writes poetry about the most unusual things such as string, Luton, Romans, glasses, buses and trains. In this selection we will look at poems that explore poetry and dogs! Hegley gives live performances and often can be heard on radio. He has even been spotted on television – so watch out.

Before you read

1   What qualities do you think should be found within a poem?

2   What was the last poem you chose to read for yourself?

3   Do you think that there is any place for poetry in our world?

Reading for meaning 1: *Poetry*

When you have read the poem, answer the following questions.

1   Select two things that a poem is or can be according to Hegley. Does this poem match your description?

2   Where does Hegley find poetry in everyday life?

3   Hegley enjoys the way poetry can make you see and understand things in a new way. He puts this into practice in this poem in the way he uses informal and **non-standard English** when you might be expecting poetry to be very formal. Find two examples of his playful use of non-standard English and explain what effect is achieved.

Standard English is the accepted language of public communication, which follows commonly accepted rules or conventions of vocabulary choice, spelling, punctuation and grammar. It does not use slang, outdated or regional language forms.

1 **Poetry**

poetry don't have to be
living in a library
there's poetry that you can see
in the life of everybody,
a lick of paint's   5
the kind of thing I mean
a lick of paint's a lovely piece of writing
the tongue of the paintbrush
giving something drab
a dab new sheen   10
a lick of paint's exciting.

there are folk who like to see
Latin in their poetry
and plenty of obscurity
me for instance   15
(only joking)
how I like to listen to the lingo
in bingo
legs eleven
clickety   20
click
a lick of paint
no – sorry that ain't one

poetry – language on a spree
I want to be   25
a leaf on the poetree
poetry is good for me
I think I'll have some for my tea

2 My doggie don't wear glasses

my doggie don't wear glasses
so they're lying when they say
a dog looks like its owner
aren't they

3 Memory

my sister loved animals
she was always taking the dog out
and stroking it
and the goldfish

Reading for meaning 2: *My doggie don't wear glasses*

● In this poem Hegley uses the cliché that owners look like their dogs. What effect is achieved by the change he makes to this cliché?

> A **cliché** is a phrase that may once have been original and striking but has become so over-used that it no longer conveys any strength of feeling or opinion.

Reading for meaning 3: *Memory*

Look again at the title of the poem. Why do you think Hegley has called his poem M*emory*?

4 A comparison of logs and dogs

both are very popular at Christmas
but it is not generally considered cruel
to abandon a log
and dogs are rarely used as fuel

5 In the arms of my glasses

they can call me softy
as ofty
as they please
but still I'll stand by these
my little optical accessories
they stop me walking into lamp-posts
and trees
when it's foggy
and I'm out walking with my doggy

Reading for meaning 4: *A comparison of logs and dogs*

1 As the title says, this poem works around an unusual comparison. The first line draws the comparison. At what point does it stop and how does Hegley signal this to his reader?

2 What is gained by the image in this poem?

Reading for meaning 5: *In the arms of my glasses*

1 Who do you think the 'they' is in the first line of this poem?

2 Titles seem to be important to the way in which the whole poem works for Hegley. What are the different layers of meaning in the title here?

⑥ Flea Poem

Dog's back.
Itch
itch
scratch
scratch   5
scratch
scratch
scratch
scratch
pause   10

itch
scratch
scratch
itch
paws   15
scratch
scratch
scratch
scratch
scratch   20
scratch
scratch
scratch
scratch
scratch scratch scratch   25
bald patch.

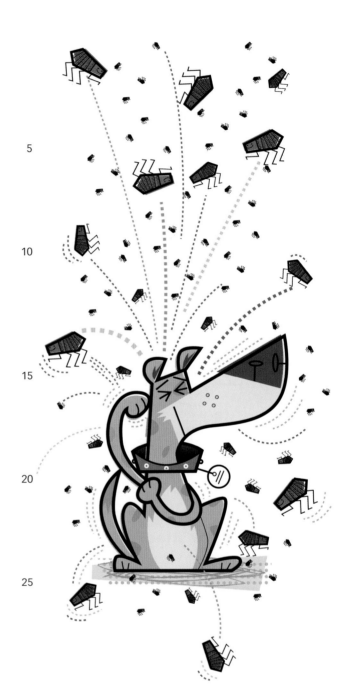

Reading for meaning 6: *Flea Poem*

1 How does the shape of this poem help to convey its meaning?

2 How important is sound in this poem? Think about the use of **onomatopoeia** and repetition.

Hegley's language and technique

You can use any of the poems you have read as examples to help answer the questions below.

1 Hegley often uses **internal rhyme** in his poetry. Pick out two examples of internal rhyme and comment on why you like them. What effect did they have when you first read the lines?

> **Internal rhyme** describes the placing of two or more words that rhyme in the same line of a poem. An example from 'Poetry' is 'poetry – language on a spree'.

2 a) In many of Hegley's poems there is little or no punctuation. What is the effect of having no capital letters at the beginning of lines in 'Poetry'?

b) Choose another poem and comment on the omission of full stops.

3 Hegley seems to like to play with words. Sometimes he changes them or even invents new ones to create the effect he wants in a poem. Can you find two examples of this in the poems you have read and explain why he chooses to alter or invent these words? How does this playfulness affect you as a reader?

4 The last line of a poem can turn the rest of the poem on its head. Scan the poems you have read to review the way in which Hegley uses last lines to create an impact. *Hint:* 'Flea poem' *or* 'Memory' *might be good places to start.*

Writing to imagine, explore and entertain

1 Many of Hegley's poems are about things close to his heart like dogs, transport, family, glasses and his home town of Luton. What subject is familiar to you that you would want to write about in poetry?

2 a) Write a poem about a subject close to your heart. In your poem, use at least one of the techniques you have been reading and learning about.

When planning your poem, think about:

changing clichés; sounds – rhyme, onomatopoeia, invented words; surprising endings; contradictions and comparisons; shape and punctuation.

b) Share this with a small group, or read it to the whole class. Make them laugh!

Writing to analyse, comment and review

Imagine you have been commissioned to write a review of Hegley's poems to be broadcast on radio for younger listeners at 7 p.m. Choose two or more poems from this selection to review.

When planning you should:

- devise an engaging and original opening that will attract your target audience

- select language that will clearly emphasise Hegley's qualities

- use **discourse markers** to link points and give coherence to the review

- use **standard English**, but remember to give your own opinion in a lively and enthusiastic way.

> **Discourse markers** are phrases, such as 'therefore', 'however', 'on the contrary', 'similarly', that help a reader or listener to understand and to follow the main line of thought or argument. They can help you when you are organising your writing into paragraphs and show that you have taken time to think about the structure of the whole text you are creating.

Drama

1 In pairs, perform one of Hegley's poems. Think about:

pace of delivery; gaps on the page and how to translate them into performance; punctuation; which words to emphasise or push; how to convey Hegley's humour to your audience.

2 Find a piece of music that you feel would be a good background sound to the radio review you wrote as a writing activity. Using two tape recorders record your broadcast.

Hunter Trials

John Betjeman was Poet Laureate for twelve years and is best remembered for his poems, although he did write scripts for film and TV and was often to be heard on radio. Betjeman came from a privileged background and his poems retell events and experiences from his life, often commenting on social habits from his observations.

Before you read

Sports, hobbies or interests often have a whole language or vocabulary associated with them. Football fans talk about 'offside', 'four – four – two formations' and 'red cards'. Tennis players talk about 'net', ' forehand', 'ace' and 'smash'.

1 Discuss with a partner any interest or hobby you have and the language associated with it.

   With whom do you use this particular vocabulary?

Hunter Trials

It's awf'lly bad luck on Diana,
Her ponies have swallowed their bits;
She fished down their throats with a spanner
  And frightened them all into fits.

So now she's attempting to borrow.   5
  Do lend her some bits, Mummy, *do*;
I'll lend her my own for tomorrow,
  But today *I*'ll be wanting them too.

Just look at Prunella on Guzzle,
  The wizardest pony on earth;   10
Why doesn't she slacken his muzzle
  And tighten the breech in his girth?

I say, Mummy, there's Mrs Geyser
  And doesn't she look pretty sick?
I bet it's because Mona Lisa   15
  Was hit on the hock with a brick.

Miss Blewitt says Monica threw it,
  But Monica says it was Joan,
And Joan's very thick with Miss Blewitt,
  So Monica's sulking alone.   20

And Margaret failed in her paces,
  Her withers got tied in a noose,
So her coronets caught in the traces
  And now all her fetlocks are loose.

Oh, it's me now. I'm terribly nervous.   25
  I wonder if Smudges will shy.
She's practically certain to swerve as
  Her Pelham is over one eye.

                  * * *

Oh wasn't it naughty of Smudges?
  Oh, Mummy, I'm sick with disgust.   30
She threw me in front of the Judges,
And my silly old collarbone's bust.

187

Reading for meaning

1　How would you describe the humour in 'Hunter Trials'?

2　a)　Do you think Betjeman likes this sport and the people he writes about in his poem?

　　b)　If not, then how do you know this and what was Betjeman hoping to achieve?

3　Look carefully at what has happened to each of the horses in this poem. Are you amused by what has befallen them?

4　Now look at what has happened to the girl who is speaking. What was your reaction to her at the end of the poem? Why?

5　What is your first impression of Betjeman's attitude to the topic of his poem and how is this idea developed as the poem progresses? *Hint: Look at the names he has chosen for the horses.*

> **Satire** describes what a writer or speaker is doing when they criticise in a humorous way. Writers often ridicule or make fun of other people's foolishness, vanity, or hypocrisy. Satire can be directed against one person or a particular group of people who have things in common.

Vocabulary and style

1　a)　Scan the poem for words that are specific to horse trials. Decide what you think each word means. Check them in a dictionary.

　　b)　How many of these words are you familiar with? Why do you think Betjeman used such specific vocabulary?

2　Describe the **rhythm** and **rhyme schemes** Betjeman uses in this poem. Are they simple or complex patterns? What effect do rhyme and rhythm have on your overall view of the poem? Use the teaching box to help you if you need to revise rhyme and rhythm.

Rhythm is the pattern of long and short, or strong and weak, beats in a line of poetry. The word 'hunter'consists of a long/strong syllable followed by a short/weak syllable.

To show such beats you can place marks over the syllables as in the following examples:

summer   beautiful   diana

Rhyme is the word used to describe similarity of sound between words or **syllables** and is often used at the end of lines in poetry, though it can be used within a line (look at John Hegley's poems for examples of this **internal rhyme**). Rhyme at the end of lines can form a pattern that may be regular or irregular. **Regular rhyme** can be used to make a poem easy to remember, to link important words, to emphasise a word, to create surprise, or humour. Here is an example of how to write out a rhyme pattern:

Peas

I eat my peas with **honey**	a
I've done it all my **life**	b
It makes the peas taste **funny**	a
But it keeps them on the **knife**	b

When you **scan** a text you aim to sweep your eyes across it quickly in order to search for something in particular. You could think of your eyes working like radar, sweeping a page of a key word or phrase.

Speaking and listening

In groups of four or six debate the motion: 'This house believes that horse trials are an enjoyable and productive activity for young people.'

- Half the group will speak for the motion and half will speak against it.

- Choose one person to deliver the case for or against the motion.

- The other members of the group will listen to the speaker presenting the opposite point of view. The group should prepare questions for the speaker at the end of his or her presentation.

- The rest of the class will decide who is the most convincing and persuasive speaker, giving their reasons.

> **Rhetorical questions** are ones that you ask when you don't expect an answer or know already that the question can't be answered. Speakers use them to make their audience feel as if they are being spoken to directly. A rhetorical question can also make the audience think about important ideas or issues and can challenge the assumptions an audience might have.

Tips on preparing your speech

A good speaker will try to:

involve his/her listener by arousing their emotions

use facts to persuade people to their point of view – think about statistics

employ colourful language to capture and maintain interest

use humour

offer **rhetorical questions** to challenge their listener

remember the importance of facial expression and gesture

think about how the volume, tone and pace of delivery can create effects

---

4.3　Writing for young children

Roald Dahl was born in Wales in 1916, though his parents were Norwegian. He worked in Africa for some time and fought in the Second World War as an RAF fighter pilot. Young children and adults read Roald Dahl's stories across the world.

The BFG

In this famous novel, Dahl tells the story of a little girl, Sophie, who is snatched from her bed one night by 'a very mixed up giant', the BFG (Big Friendly Giant). They become friends very quickly and plan to save the world from the human bean-eating giants. In this chapter, the BFG tells Sophie what he eats instead of human beans.

Before you read

1　This story is for children younger than you. What other fiction do you know with magical or strange creatures or people who make friends with young children?

2　In this chapter you will find many words Roald Dahl has invented. What other examples of nonsense writing do you know? You might have read some nonsense poetry.

3　Do you or your family use words you have invented? Share them with your partner.

Snozzcumbers

'But if you don't eat people like all the others,' Sophie said, 'then what *do* you live on?'

'That is a squelching tricky problem around here,' the BFG answered. 'In this sloshflunking Giant Country, happy eats like pineapples and pigwinkles is simply not growing. Nothing is growing except for one extremely icky-poo vegetable. It is called the snozzcumber.'

'The snozzcumber!' cried Sophie. 'There's no such thing.'

The BFG looked at Sophie and smiled, showing about twenty of his square white teeth. 'Yesterday,' he said, 'we was not believing in giants, was we? Today we is not believing in snozzcumbers. Just because we happen not to have actually *seen* something with our own two little winkles, we think it is not existing. What about for instance the great squizzly scotch-hopper?'

'I beg your pardon?' Sophie said.

'And the humplecrimp?'

'What's that?' Sophie said.

'And the wraprascal?'

'The what?' Sophie said.

'And the crumpscoddle?'

'Are they animals?' Sophie asked.

'They is *common* animals,' said the BFG contemptuously. 'I is not a very know-all giant myself, but it seems to me that you is an absolutely know-nothing human bean. Your brain is full of rotten-wool.'

'You mean cottonwool,' Sophie said.

'What I mean and what I say is two different things,' the BFG announced rather grandly. 'I will now show you a snozzcumber.'

The BFG flung open a massive cupboard and took out the weirdest-looking thing Sophie had ever seen. It was about half as long again as an ordinary man but was much thicker. It was as thick around its girth as a perambulator. It was black with white stripes along its length. And it was covered all over with coarse knobbles.

'Here is the repulsant snozzcumber!' cried the BFG, waving it about. 'I squoggle it! I mispise it! I dispunge it! But because I is refusing to gobble up human beans like the other giants, I must spend my life guzzling up icky-poo snozzcumbers instead. If I don't, I will be nothing but skin and groans.'

'You mean skin and *bones*,' Sophie said.

'I know it is bones,' the BFG said. 'But please understand that I cannot be helping it if I sometimes is saying things a little squiggly. *I* is trying my very best all the time.' The Big Friendly Giant looked suddenly so forlorn that Sophie got quite upset.

'I'm sorry,' she said. 'I didn't mean to be rude.'

'There never was any schools to teach me talking in Giant Country,' the BFG said sadly.

'But couldn't your mother have taught you?' Sophie asked.

'My *mother*!' cried the BFG. 'Giants don't have mothers! Surely you is knowing *that*.'

'I did not know that,' Sophie said.

'Whoever heard of a *woman* giant!' shouted the BFG, waving the snozzcumber around his head like a lasso. 'There never was a woman giant! And there never will be one. Giants is always men!'

Sophie felt herself getting a little muddled. 'In that case,' she said, 'how were you born?'

'Giants isn't born,' the BFG answered. 'Giants *appears* and that's all there is to it. They simply *appears*, the same way as the sun and the stars.'

'And when did you appear?' Sophie asked.

'Now how on earth could I be knowing anything like that?' said the BFG. 'It was so long ago I couldn't count.'

'You mean you don't even know how *old* you are?'

'No giant is knowing that,' the BFG said. 'All I is knowing about myself is that I is very old, very very old and crumply. Perhaps as old as the earth.'

What happens when a giant dies?' Sophie asked.

'Giants is never dying,' the BFG answered. 'Sometimes and quite suddenly, a giant is disappearing and nobody is ever knowing where he goes to. But mostly us giants is simply going on and on like whiffsy time-twiddlers.'

The BFG was still holding the awesome snozzcumber in his right hand, and now he put one end into his mouth and bit off a huge hunk of it. He started crunching it up and the noise he made was like the crunching of lumps of ice.

'It's filthing!' he spluttered, speaking with his mouth full and spraying large pieces of snozzcumber like bullets in Sophie's direction. Sophie hopped around on the table-top, ducking out of the way.

'It's disgusterous!' the BFG gurgled. 'It's sickable! It's rotsome! It's maggotwise! Try it yourself, this foulsome snozzcumber!'

'No, thank you,' Sophie said, backing away.

'It's all you're going to be guzzling around here from now on so you might as well get used to it,' said the BFG. 'Go on, you snipsy little winkle, have a go!'

Sophie took a small nibble. 'Uggggggggh!' she spluttered. 'Oh no! Oh gosh! Oh help!' She spat it out quickly. 'It tastes of frogskins!' she gasped. 'And rotten fish!'

'Worse than that!' cried the BFG, roaring with laughter. 'To me it is tasting of clockcoaches and slime-wanglers!'

'Do we really have to eat it?' Sophie said.

'You do unless you is wanting to become so thin you will be disappearing into a thick ear.'

'Into *thin air*,' Sophie said. 'A thick ear is something quite different.'

Once again that sad winsome look came into the BFG's eyes. 'Words,' he said, 'is oh such a twitch-tickling problem to me all my life. So you must simply try to be patient and stop squibbling. As I am telling you before, I know exactly what words I am wanting to say, but somehow or other they is always getting squiff-squaddled around.'

'That happens to everyone,' Sophie said.

'Not like it happens to me,' the BFG said. 'I is speaking the most terrible wigglish.'

'I think you speak beautifully,' Sophie said.

'You do?' cried the BFG, suddenly brightening. 'You really do?'

'Simply beautifully,' Sophie repeated.

'Well, that is the nicest present anybody is ever giving me in my whole life!' cried the BFG. 'Are you sure you is not twiddling my leg?'

'Of course not,' Sophie said. 'I just love the way you talk.'

'How wondercrump!' cried the BFG, still beaming. 'How whoopsey-splunkers! How absolutely squiffling! I is all of a stutter.'

'Listen,' Sophie said. 'We don't *have* to eat snozzcumbers. In the fields around our village there are all sorts of lovely vegetables like cauliflowers and carrots. Why don't you get some of those next time you go visiting?'

The BFG raised his great head proudly in the air. 'I is a very honourable giant,' he said. 'I would rather be chewing up rotsome snozzcumbers than snitching things from other people.'

'You stole *me*,' Sophie said.

'I did not steal you very much,' said the BFG, smiling gently. 'After all, you is only a tiny little girl.'

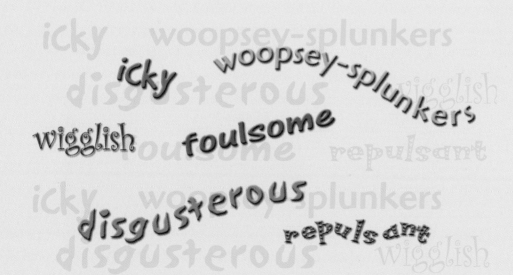

Reading for meaning

I How does Dahl make the characters appealing for his young readers?

2 The BFG is much older than Sophie and yet she seems to take on the role of an adult rather than a child.

   a) How does Sophie help the BFG. What does this say about their relationship?

   b) Is there anything funny about this role reversal?

Vocabulary and language variation

I The BFG speaks very differently to Sophie. He knows this himself, as he says:

> 'But please understand that I cannot be helping it if I sometimes *is* saying things a little squiggly. I *is* trying my best all the time.'

Later, he explains that he has never been to school and that he didn't have a mum to teach him to speak. He says:

> 'Words *is* oh such a twitch-tickling problem to me all my life. So you must simply try to be patient and stop squibbling. As I am telling you before, I know exactly what words I am wanting to say, but somehow or other they *is* always getting squiff-squaddled around.'

Look at the verbs italicised in the quotation above. What rule is he getting wrong?

2 Sometimes the BFG mixes up his words. Look at the examples below, scan the chapter to find them in context and explain where his mistakes lie. Why might this be funny? *Hint: It might help you to think about how these words sound.*

BFG's word	Mistake
rotton-wool	
skin and groans	
clockcoaches	
thick ear	
wigglish	

3 Many of the words that the BFG says are nonsense words and yet his sentences still make some sense to the reader and we know what he means.

a) Look at the table below and complete it with the proper words you think would best replace the BFG's words if you were to 'translate' them.

BFG's word	English
repulsant	
icky	
disgusterous	
foulsome	
wigglish	
whoopsey-splunkers	

b) How did you know how to translate the words?

4 What kind of words have you used to replace the ones spoken by the BFG? Are these the only type of words he invents?

5 Think again about the background information you were given at the start of this unit. Why do you think Roald Dahl has the BFG talk in jumbled sentences using made-up words? What effect does this achieve?

Writing to imagine, explore and entertain

1 Write a short piece where the BFG goes on a trip to Sophie's world. Try to write using the vocabulary and style of Roald Dahl, thinking carefully about the way in which the BFG speaks and the words he uses. You should invent some nonsense words of your own. *Hint: Don't forget that this text is for younger children.*

2 Now, imagine Sophie takes the BFG to the zoo. Write a description of their trip. Think about what he might call the animals and how he might describe their behaviour.

Review

Which text did you enjoy reading in his chapter? Why did it appeal to you?

Which activity did you find most challenging? Did you enjoy it?

What do you know now that you didn't know before you began your study of humour?

How would you evaluate your performance on the speaking and listening tasks?

Use this checklist to help you answer these questions and to review the progress you have made.

- **You have read:** a range of modern poems; extracts from a medieval poem; extracts from a modern adult novel; a chapter from a modern children's novel; and a selection of scenes from a Shakespeare play.

- **You have thought about how writers use:** rhyme, rhythm, alliteration, repetition, onomatopoeia, slang and careful word choice to achieve particular effects; sentence construction and punctuation to control the reader's experience; nonsense words.

- **You have written to:** imagine, explore and entertain – a poem, a diary, a story; inform, explain and describe – a descriptive narrative of a trip, a short piece of humorous description; persuade, argue and advise – an article; analyse, review and comment – an analysis of language effects in a play, a review of poetry.

- **To improve your writing you have explored:** sentence length and structure, questions and commands; a range of punctuation; verbs and adjectives; formal and informal language and how to surprise your reader with twists and contrasts.

- **Your speaking and listening work has included:** discussing texts with a partner and in class; performing a poem; improvisation and scripting character dialogue; rehearsal and performance of lines from a play; work on spoken Middle English.

- **You may have used ICT to:** research the festival of Twelfth Night; find out about Chaucer and medieval England; spellcheck and present final drafts of your written work; record your performances for analysis.

5 Science fiction

Science fiction is often thought of as fantasy writing, but usually involves imagining what life might be like on other planets, or what life could be like in our world in the future.

Think of as many science fiction stories or TV programmes as you can.

Science fiction often explores the possibility of better medical knowledge, or the benefits (or dangers) of increased scientific knowledge. Why do you think people enjoy reading science fiction?

5.1 Life in space

The First Men on Mercury

The first text in this chapter is a poem written by Edwin Morgan. It is a science fiction poem about men landing on the planet Mercury.

Before you read

1 Do you believe that there is life on other planets?

2 What sort of places do you imagine other planets to be?

3 What would be the problems of trying to live with beings from a different planet?

Reading for meaning

1 Why have the Earthmen come to Mercury?

2 a) What do the Mercurians tell the Earthmen to do?

   b) What do you think their reasons are?

3 What do you think the Earthmen have gained by being on Mercury?

4 a) How does the writer create the effect of the Earthmen and the Mercurians learning each other's language?

   b) Where in the poem do you notice this?

5 a) To what extent can you work out what the Mercurian language means? How can you do this?

   b) What is the effect of not being able to understand?

   c) What is the effect of using the following techniques:

   ● quotation marks

   ● exclamation marks

   ● question marks?

6 How does the writer structure the poem?

The First Men on Mercury

– We come in peace from the third planet.
Would you take us to your leader?

– Bawr stretter! Bawr. Bawr. Stretterhawl?

– This is a little plastic model
of the solar system, with working parts.   5
You are here and we are there and we
are now here with you, is this clear?

– Gawl horrop. Bawr. Abawrhannahanna!

– Where we come from is blue and white
with brown, you see we call the brown   10
here 'land', the blue is 'sea', and the white
is 'clouds' over land and sea, we live
on the surface of the brown land,
all round is sea and clouds. We are 'men'.
Men come –   15

Glawp men! Gawrbenner menko. Menhawl?

– Men come in peace from the third planet
which we call 'earth'. We are earthmen.
Take us earthmen to your leader.

– Thmen? Thmen? Bawr. Bawrhossop.   20
Yuleeda tan henna. Harrabost yuleeda.

202

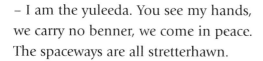

– I am the yuleeda. You see my hands,
we carry no benner, we come in peace.
The spaceways are all stretterhawn.

– Glawn peacemen all horrabhanna tantko!   25
Tan come at'mstrossop. Glawp yuleeda!

– Atoms are peacegawl in our harraban.
Menbat worrabost from tan hannahanna.

– You men we know bawrhossoptant. Bawr.
We know yuleeda. Go strawg backspetter quick.   30

– We cantantabawr, tantingko backspetter now!

– Banghapper now! Yes, third planet back.
Yuleeda will go back blue, white, brown
nowhanna! There is no more talk.

– Gaw! han fasthapper   35

– No. You must go back to your planet.
Go back in peace, take what you have gained
but quickly.

– Stretterworra gawl, gawl …

– Of course, but nothing is ever the same   40
now is it? You'll remember Mercury.

Vocabulary and spelling

1 In pairs, work out what you think the Mercurian words mean. Say why you decided on the meaning. Think about how the words sound and how they are spelt. Are there any other clues in the text to help you? Think about the situation or context. There may be more than one answer.

2 Compile a phrase book with English translations of the Mercurian words from the poem.

Writing to imagine, explore and entertain

1 Working in pairs, invent your own language from another planet. Write a poem using Morgan's as a model. You might like to do the following:

● adapt the first two lines of Morgan's poems, for example:

I/We come in peace from ...

Our names are ...

● write the 'other' language in **standard English** first, then change it to your invented language.

● with your partner, compose the poem orally, then write it down.

2 Perform your poem to the rest of the class.

3 Illustrate your poem for display.

The Keeper of the Isis Light

This extract comes from 'The Keeper of the Isis Light' by American, Monica Hughes. The beautiful planet of Isis is to be colonised by a group of settlers from Earth. Olwen welcomes them. Her parents were also from Earth, but died when Olwen was a young child. She now lives alone with her protector, Guardian. In this extract, Guardian has been telling Olwen about her parents, and is about to reveal how he has changed her body by **genetic engineering** to ensure her survival.

Before you read

What problems do you think humans might have adapting to life on another planet? You might like to think about how you would cope if you were travelling through hostile places on Earth, for example the desert or the North Pole. Think about how modern technology might help you.

A **gene** is a material within the nucleus of a cell which controls the development of the qualities of a living thing – and is passed on from its parent. Your genes determine, for example, your height and whether you have blue or brown eyes.

Genetic engineering is when a creature is changed by artificial alteration of its genes.

The Keeper of the Isis Light

Again the silence hung heavily in the room. Olwen shivered. Then Guardian spoke. "I changed you. At first I took away your memory, so that you would not grieve for the loss of your parents. Then, little by little, surgically and genetically, I changed you."

"Changed . . . ?"

"Humans are so frail, so poorly adapted." Guardian's voice was almost angry. "There were a thousand things on Isis that could have killed you when you were a child, too small to understand the dangers. I could not guard you every second. I had my duties to the Light. And you could not have been happy as a prisoner, I was sure of that. So I adapted you to Isis. I thickened your skin so that it would be opaque to the ultraviolet. I gave you an extra eye-lid to protect your eyes—Ra is so much brighter than Earth's sun."

Olwen's hands crept up to her face. Guardian went on. "I deepened your rib-cage and extended your vascular system, much in the way that the deep-sea mammals adapted theirs, so that you could store much more oxygen at each breath. I widened your nostrils too, to help you breathe more fully.

"Anything else?"

"I strengthened your ankles and thickened your fingernails to help you climb. And I changed your metabolism slightly . . . that shows in your altered skin colour."

"Why?"

"So that the poisonous plants and insects of Isis could not harm you."

"You did all that for me?"

"And for your mother. It was her command."

"She must have loved me very much, to be thinking only of me when she was dying."

"Oh, she did, Olwen. And so did your father." "And you, Guardian . . . do you love me?"

I . . . you . . . you are my reason," he stammered. "You are not angry with me?"

"Why should I be? You gave me freedom. You gave me happiness. You gave me Isis. I love you for it, Guardian."

"Thank you." He bowed his head slightly, and for a second seemed almost overcome.

"What I don't understand is that you should feel guilty for what you did for me," Olwen said at last.

"What I did . . ." He stopped and then began again. "You have to understand something difficult. What I did has made you very different from other Earthtype people . . . different from all the settlers . . . different from Mark."

"I know. I've already noticed. I'm better. I'm not confined to

UVO suits and oxygen masks. And I am strong. Much stronger than Mark. Guardian!" She stared at him. "Is that why you made me that ridiculous suit and mask? It had nothing to do with viruses—Dr MacDonald was right about that—you were hiding me from the settlers. You didn't want them to see me. Why?"

"I had a plan. I had hoped that you would all get to know each other slowly. That you would learn first to trust, to become friends. Then I hoped that the differences between you would no longer be so important."

"But they're not . . . not to me!" Olwen drew in a sharp breath and looked down at her own hands. They were what they had always been, familiar, comfortable extensions of herself. Was there anything wrong with her hands? "Guardian, is that why there are no mirrors? Were you afraid that I couldn't even bear to look at myself. Am I . . . horrible?"

"No, no. It is nothing like that. Oh dear, perhaps that was another wrong decision. It is so difficult to gauge a person's emotional reactions, even a person whom I know as well as I know you. But I thought that if you were as familiar with your own appearance as having a mirrored companion might make you, that then you might be afraid of the settlers, since you would perceive how different they are from you."

"Am I . . . am I very different?"

"Yes."

"Am I ugly?"

"No! You are not ugly at all. Form and function should be as one. You function perfectly. You are beautiful."

Olwen stood up. "My head is spinning. It is too much all at once. Mark. Hobbit. And now a mother, a father, a past and a new body . . . I think I must be by myself for a while. Will you do something for me right away?"

"Of course."

"Make a mirror for my room. A big one, please, so that I can see all of myself at once. And can you make it so that I can see the different sides of myself? Can you do that?"

"I will see to it right away. You understand, I did not want you to have a mirror before, but now that you know about yourself ..."

She nodded. "I'll be on the terrace." She walked out of the cold, strangely inhuman room where Guardian spent so much of his time and into the living room. The scent of cactus flower still lingered in the air, although it was many hours since she had thrown the golden flower into the incinerator. When she walked out onto the terrace the scent became even more powerful, and she realised that it was being wafted to her on the evening breeze from the eastern mountain. The whole upper slope, above the grassline, was a mass of blooming cactus.

She could no more rid Isis of the scent than she could rid herself of her feelings towards Mark. Unless she made Guardian fire the whole mountainside and destroy the flowers. He would do it if she were to ask him. He would take away the memory of her love for Mark, too, if she were to ask it of him.

She walked to the edge of the terrace and looked across the river valley. To do violence to the mountains and the creatures that lived there, just because she could not bear the scent of the cactus flower, would be hideously wrong. To do violence to her mind, so as to forget her unhappiness, would be equally wrong.

Something strange was beginning to happen inside her. Little memories were swelling up inside her mind and bursting into tiny disassociated glimpses of reality. There were warm hands, strong and gentle, and the feeling of someone tickling her chest with a bearded chin, and the sound of laughter. Her laughter.

She began to understand why Hobbit had meant so much to her. Hobbit was warm, alive, huggable. And that was necessary… or had been necessary. She had the painful feeling that she was growing inside so fast that she was going to split and shed her skin, the way a snake does. She could remember laughter… Guardian had been so good to her, he had been everything to her. Only Guardian never laughed.

She shut her eyes, the better to endure the waves of emotion that shook her. The only other reality was the rough stone of the balustrade under the grip of her fingers. She was still standing there under the starlight when Guardian came out to tell her that the mirror had been installed in her room. She bent her head in acknowledgement and walked swiftly past him, wrapped in her own thoughts. Guardian's eyes followed her with an expression that on anyone else might have been mistaken for sorrow or regret.

As soon as Olwen entered her room, sweeping aside the curtain that covered the door arch, she saw the Other standing, one arm holding the window curtain, about to move towards her. She stopped abruptly, her heart jolting, suddenly angry. Nobody came here. This was her own most private place.

"Who are you?" she snapped, and it seemed that the Other's lips moved mockingly. She walked forward, letting the door curtain fall behind her. Across the wide carpet the Other came to meet her.

Halfway across the room she understood. This was a mirror! The Other, the intruder, was herself. She walked towards herself and touched the surface of the mirror. It was cold and hard; and behind her she could see the whole room crowded into its flatness. As her finger reached out, so did the Other's finger, and, at the cold surface of the glass, they touched.

Olwen had always imagined that a mirror would reflect the same kind of faulty image that she had seen when she had squatted by a rain puddle when she was small, or looked at her fat upside-down face in the bowl of a polished spoon. But this was quite different. This was almost as alive as she was.

She stared at herself, pushing her red hair away from her face. She had nice bones, she decided, a bit lumpy above the eyes to protect her from the sun, with wide nostrils and a big rib-cage to make the most use of the thin air. She was much more serviceable than the narrow-chested, pinch-faced people from Earth.

Remembering Mark's freckles and the flushed peeling skin that she had noticed on the fairer settlers, she peered at her own skin, and then slipped out of her dressing gown so that she could see all of herself. Her body was strong and smooth, with no freckles or raw places or other deformities, but a nice bronzy green all over. She knew its colour—after all she could see bits of herself every time she stripped—but she had not realised what a striking contrast the bronze made to her red hair. She turned and pirouetted in front of the mirror so that her hair swirled out in a cloud around her.

A tiny reflection from the bedside lamp caught in the glass and shone directly into her eyes, and at once, without her conscious will, a nictating membrane slid over her blue eyes, like a gauze blind. She moved, so that the light no longer shone directly into her eyes, and at once it quickly slid out of sight behind her lower eye-lid. Neat, she thought, and moved so that it happened again.

Olwen turned the side panels of the mirror so that she could see every scrap of herself, and finally she dressed and went back to the living room. Guardian was standing by the fireplace. He looked as if he had not moved since she had left him. All these years he's served me, she thought, planned and schemed to make my life good and happy, and never once has he asked for anything in return. On a sudden wave of gratitude she ran across the room and caught his arms. "Dear Guardian, thank you for my body. It's beautiful!"

He looked down at her, his face expressionless. "You are not angry at what I did?"

"Angry? Why should I be angry? You kept me safe. You gave me a better life than these colonists will ever know. You gave me Isis—the mountains as well as the valleys. I love you for it, Guardian … thank you."

Reading for meaning

1 Why does Guardian feel it was necessary to alter Olwen's body?

2 Why doesn't Olwen realise she is different from the Earth settlers?

3 How does the writer convey Olwen's positive response to her body? *Hint: Look at the language used and the choice of adjectives and verbs, as well as Olwen's actions.*

4 What reason might Olwen have had for being angry with Guardian?

5 a) What does this sentence mean?

'… and at once, without her conscious will, a nictating membrane slid over her blue eyes.'

b) What does Guardian mean when he says:

'Form and function should be as one'?

Sentences and punctuation

1 What do you notice about the sentences in the opening four lines of this extract? *Hint: Are they simple or complex? Long or short? What is the effect created?*

2 Look at the three paragraphs from the section beginning 'She nodded. "I'll be on the terrace."' What recurring image connects these paragraphs?

3 Why does the writer start a new paragraph each time Olwen and Guardian reply to each other?

Vocabulary

1 In pairs, list ten words and phrases that identify the text as science fiction. *Hint: Think about scientific, biological and space related words.*

2 a) How many aspects of Olwen's body have been changed?

b) Explain the meaning of **metabolism** and **vascular system**. You may want to look in a dictionary first.

211

Drama

1   Mime Olwen's actions and behaviour from the moment she enters the room with the mirror, to when she pirouettes.

2   In pairs, devise a role-play in which Olwen and a settler from Earth see each other for the first time. Discuss how the settler would react to Olwen's appearance before you act out the role-play.

Speaking and listening

Genetic engineering is a topical issue. Split into three groups and prepare a debate about the pros and cons of genetic engineering. Think about:

- eradication of hereditary diseases

- increased availability of organs for transplant

- safer cosmetic surgery

- the issue of 'designer' babies; everyone wanting to conform to an expected standard of appearance

- people developing a lower immunity to disease

The first group should argue for genetic engineering and the second group should argue against it. Present your arguments like a debate, making sure your presentations are no longer than two minutes. The third group should think of questions to ask each group at the end of the debate. Finish the session by voting for or against the motion.

Writing to persuade, argue and advise

Write a letter to a newspaper in which you give your opinions for or against genetic engineering. Remember the following points when writing a formal letter:

- set out your address and date correctly

- begin your letter 'Dear Sir/Madam'

- state your subject For example: 'I am writing to explain my views on genetic engineering.'

- each paragraph should explain one particular point

- use link words to connect paragraphs For example: 'furthermore', 'however', 'nevertheless'.

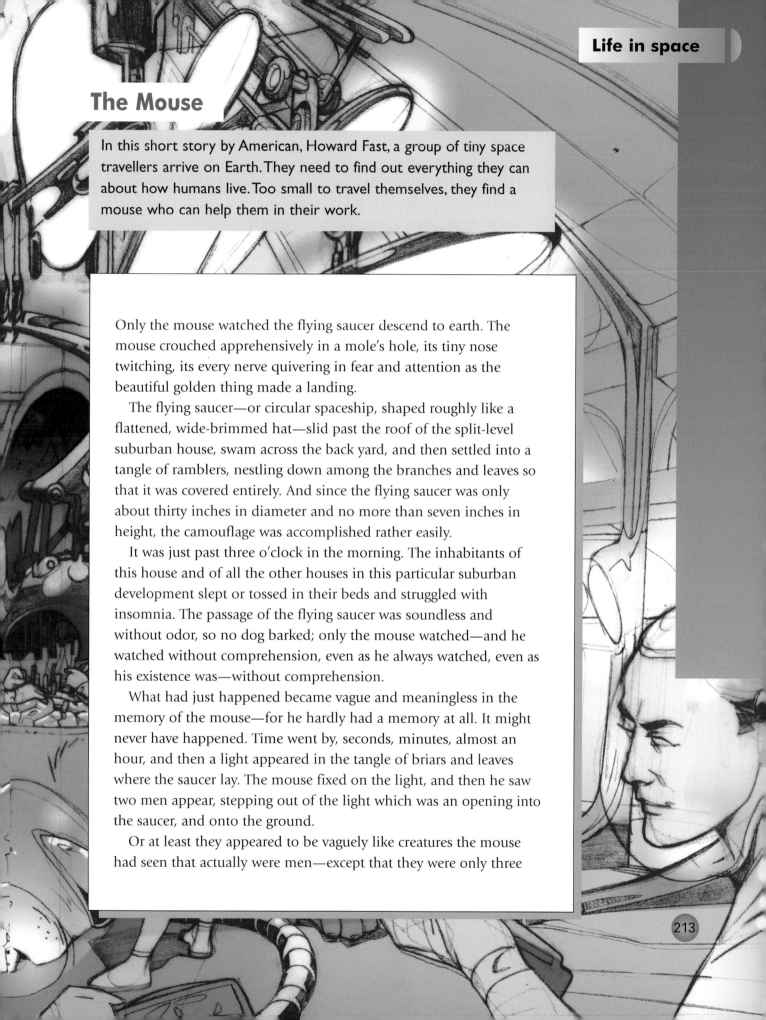

The Mouse

In this short story by American, Howard Fast, a group of tiny space travellers arrive on Earth. They need to find out everything they can about how humans live. Too small to travel themselves, they find a mouse who can help them in their work.

Only the mouse watched the flying saucer descend to earth. The mouse crouched apprehensively in a mole's hole, its tiny nose twitching, its every nerve quivering in fear and attention as the beautiful golden thing made a landing.

The flying saucer—or circular spaceship, shaped roughly like a flattened, wide-brimmed hat—slid past the roof of the split-level suburban house, swam across the back yard, and then settled into a tangle of ramblers, nestling down among the branches and leaves so that it was covered entirely. And since the flying saucer was only about thirty inches in diameter and no more than seven inches in height, the camouflage was accomplished rather easily.

It was just past three o'clock in the morning. The inhabitants of this house and of all the other houses in this particular suburban development slept or tossed in their beds and struggled with insomnia. The passage of the flying saucer was soundless and without odor, so no dog barked; only the mouse watched—and he watched without comprehension, even as he always watched, even as his existence was—without comprehension.

What had just happened became vague and meaningless in the memory of the mouse—for he hardly had a memory at all. It might never have happened. Time went by, seconds, minutes, almost an hour, and then a light appeared in the tangle of briars and leaves where the saucer lay. The mouse fixed on the light, and then he saw two men appear, stepping out of the light which was an opening into the saucer, and onto the ground.

Or at least they appeared to be vaguely like creatures the mouse had seen that actually were men—except that they were only three

inches tall and enclosed in spacesuits. If the mouse could have distinguished between the suit and what it contained and if the mouse's vision had been selective, he might have seen that under the transparent covering the men from the saucer differed only in size from the men on earth—at least in general appearance. Yet in other ways they differed a great deal. They did not speak vocally, nor did their suits contain any sort of radio equipment; they were telepaths, and after they had stood in silence for about five minutes they exchanged thoughts.

"The thing to keep in mind," said the first man, "is that while our weight is so much less here than at home, we are still very, very heavy. And this ground is not very dense."

"No, it isn't, is it? Are they all asleep?"

The first reached out. His mind became an electronic network that touched the minds of every living creature within a mile or so.

"Almost all the people are asleep. Most of the animals appear to be nocturnal."

"Curious?"

No—not really. Most of the animals are undomesticated—small, wild creatures. Great fear—hunger and fear."

"Poor things."

"Yes—poor things, yet they manage to survive. That's quite a feat, under the noses of the people. Interesting people. Probe a bit."

The second man reached out with his mind and probed. His reaction might be translated as "Ugh!"

"Yes—yes, indeed. They think some horrible thoughts, don't they? I'm afraid I prefer the animals. There's one right up ahead of us. Wide awake and with nothing else in that tiny brain of his but fear. In fact, fear and hunger seem to add up to his total mental baggage. No hate, no aggression."

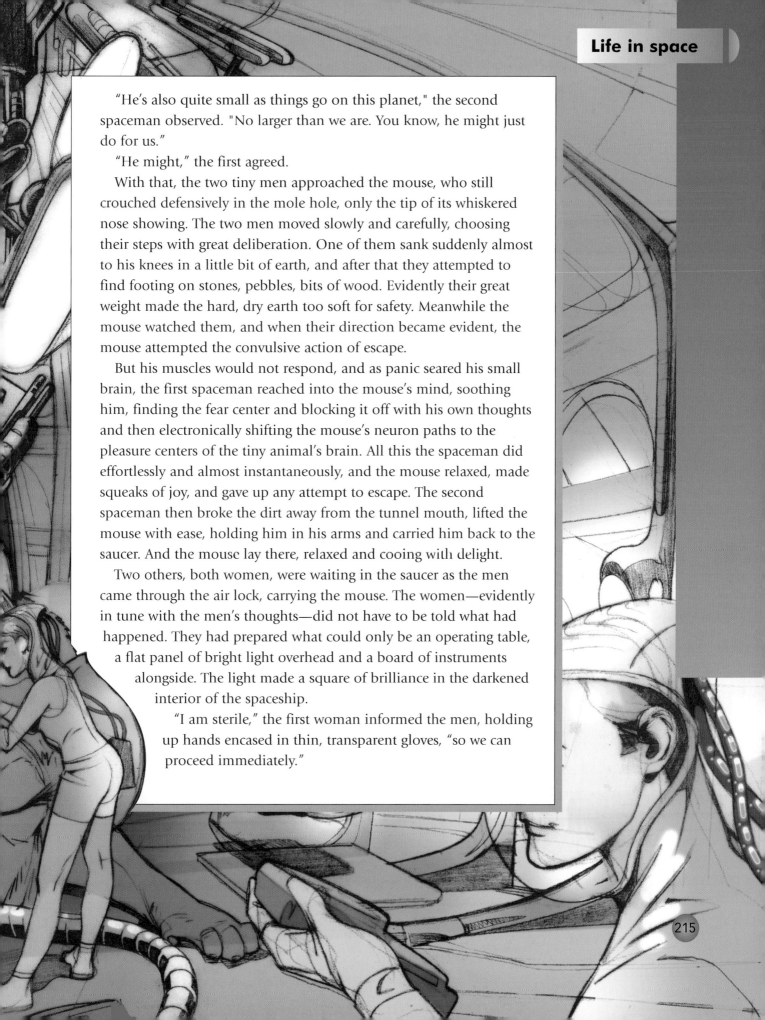

"He's also quite small as things go on this planet," the second spaceman observed. "No larger than we are. You know, he might just do for us."

"He might," the first agreed.

With that, the two tiny men approached the mouse, who still crouched defensively in the mole hole, only the tip of its whiskered nose showing. The two men moved slowly and carefully, choosing their steps with great deliberation. One of them sank suddenly almost to his knees in a little bit of earth, and after that they attempted to find footing on stones, pebbles, bits of wood. Evidently their great weight made the hard, dry earth too soft for safety. Meanwhile the mouse watched them, and when their direction became evident, the mouse attempted the convulsive action of escape.

But his muscles would not respond, and as panic seared his small brain, the first spaceman reached into the mouse's mind, soothing him, finding the fear center and blocking it off with his own thoughts and then electronically shifting the mouse's neuron paths to the pleasure centers of the tiny animal's brain. All this the spaceman did effortlessly and almost instantaneously, and the mouse relaxed, made squeaks of joy, and gave up any attempt to escape. The second spaceman then broke the dirt away from the tunnel mouth, lifted the mouse with ease, holding him in his arms and carried him back to the saucer. And the mouse lay there, relaxed and cooing with delight.

Two others, both women, were waiting in the saucer as the men came through the air lock, carrying the mouse. The women—evidently in tune with the men's thoughts—did not have to be told what had happened. They had prepared what could only be an operating table, a flat panel of bright light overhead and a board of instruments alongside. The light made a square of brilliance in the darkened interior of the spaceship.

"I am sterile," the first woman informed the men, holding up hands encased in thin, transparent gloves, "so we can proceed immediately."

215

Like the men, the women's skin was yellow, not sallow but a bright, glowing lemon yellow, the hair rich orange. Out of the spacesuits, they would all be dressed more or less alike, barefoot and in shorts in the warm interior of the ship.

"I reached out," the second woman told them. "They're all asleep, but their minds!"

"We know," the men agreed.

"I rooted around—like a journey through a sewer. But I picked up a good deal. The animal is called a mouse. It is symbolically the smallest and most harmless of creatures, vegetarian, and hunted by practically everything else on this curious planet. Only its size accounts for its survival, and its only skill is concealment."

Meanwhile the two men had laid the mouse on the operating table, where it sprawled relaxed and squeaking contentment. While the men went to change out of their spacesuits, the second woman filled a hypodermic instrument, inserted the needle near the base of the mouse's tail, and gently forced the fluid in. The mouse relaxed and became unconscious. Then the two women changed the mouse's position, handling the—to them huge—animal with ease and dispatch, as if it had almost no weight; and actually in terms of the gravitation they were built to contend with, it had almost no weight at all.

When the two men returned, they were dressed as were the women, in shorts, and barefoot, with the same transparent gloves. The four of them then began to work together, quickly, expertly—evidently a team who had worked in this manner many times in the past. The mouse now lay upon its stomach, its feet spread. One man put a cone-shaped mask over its head and began the feeding of oxygen. The other man shaved the top of its head with an electric razor, while the two women began an operation which would remove the entire top of the mouse's skull. Working with great speed and skill, they incised the skin, and then using trephines that were armed with a sort of laser beam rather than a saw, they cut through the top of the skull, removed it, and handed it to one of the men who placed it in a pan that was filled with a glowing solution. The brain of the mouse was thus exposed.

The two women then wheeled over a machine with a turret top on a universal joint, lowered the top close to the exposed brain, and pressed a button. About a hundred tiny wires emerged from the turret top, and very fast, the women began to attach these wires to parts of the mouse's brain. The man who had been controlling the oxygen flow now brought over another machine, drew tubes out of it, and began a process of feeding fluid into the mouse's circulatory system, while the second man began to work on the skull section that was in the glowing solution.

The four of them worked steadily and apparently without fatigue. Outside, the night ended and the sun rose, and still the four space people worked on. At about noon, they finished the first part of their work and stood back from the table to observe and admire what they had done. The tiny brain of the mouse had been increased fivefold in size, and in shape and folds resembled a miniature human brain. Each of the four shared a feeling of great accomplishment, and they mingled their thoughts and praised each other and then proceeded to complete the operation. The shape of the skull section that had been removed was now compatible with the changed brain, and when they replaced it on the mouse's head, the only noticeable difference in the creature's appearance was a strange, high lump above his eyes. They sealed the breaks and joined the flesh with some sort of plastic, removed the tubes, inserted new tubes, and changed the deep unconsciousness of the mouse to a deep sleep.

For the next five days the mouse slept—but from motionless sleep, its condition changed gradually, until on the fifth day it began to stir and move restlessly, and then on the sixth day it awakened. During those five days it was fed intravenously, massaged constantly, and probed constantly and telepathically. The four space people took turns at entering its mind and feeding it information, and neuron by neuron, section by section, they programmed its newly enlarged brain. They were very skilled at this. They gave the mouse background knowledge, understanding, language, and self-comprehension. They fed it a vast amount of information, balanced the information with a philosophical comprehension of the universe and its meaning, left it as it had been emotionally, without aggression or hostility, but also without fear. When the mouse finally awakened, it knew what it was and how it had become what it was. It still remained a mouse, but in the enchanting wonder and majesty of its mind, it was like no other mouse that had ever lived on the planet Earth.

Reading for meaning

1 Why was the spaceship able to land without being noticed?

2 Why do you think the writer starts the story with 'Only'?

3 In the first paragraph, Howard Fast describes the mouse crouching 'apprehensively in a mole's hole, its tiny nose twitching, its every nerve quivering in fear and attention'.

   a) What impression of the mouse does this give?

   b) Where are there links to these words later in the text? What effect do these links achieve?

4 Which words in the first two paragraphs on page 213 suggest that the spacecraft is not threatening?

5 Explain how it is possible for the space traveller to lift the mouse, even though, compared to the traveller, the mouse is so big.

6 Look at the section on page 214 beginning "The thing to keep in mind" and ending '… translated as "Ugh!" '

   What language does the writer use to show that the space travellers are communicating telepathically?

7 Why do the space travellers choose the mouse rather than a human to help them?

8 Look at the last sentence of the last paragraph. How does this reflect how the mouse has changed?

Sentences, paragraphs and punctuation

1 Look at the last sentence in paragraph three on page 213: 'The passage of the flying saucer … without comprehension'.

   a) Describe the structure of this sentence. Hint: *Think about the use of subordinate clauses, semi-colons, hyphens and sentence length.*

   b) Why has the writer used a sentence like this here? What effect does it create? Think about the meaning of the sentence.

2 Look at the paragraph beginning 'With that, the two tiny men approached the mouse' and the paragraph which follows it. How are these two paragraphs linked? *Hint: Look at what each paragraph describes, the use of a connective.*

3 Look at the paragraph at the bottom of page 216 beginning: 'When the two men returned...' to the paragraph on page 217 ending '... in the glowing solution.' What is being described and the writer's style make this an effective description? How does the use of punctuation and sentence structure create this effect?

Writing to imagine, explore and entertain

Continue writing the story from the moment the mouse wakes up. You might like to consider:

● how the space travellers ask the mouse to help them

● what the mouse does and where he goes

● his return to the space travellers and what happens to him.

Writing to explain and describe

Imagine you are one of the aliens and you have to send a news report back to your planet about the mouse. Describe the mouse's physical features and mental characteristics from the alien's perspective. Think about what would be unusual for the alien. The report should include:

● accurate information about the appearance of the mouse

● a description of the mouse's reactions and behaviour

● an explanation of why the mouse is ideal for your purposes.

Speaking and listening

Animal experimentation is a controversial subject. In groups, discuss the following questions.

1 Why did the space travellers change the mouse's brain?

2 Did they improve the mouse's life or not?

3 Did they respect the mouse or not?

4 Can what they did be morally justified?

5 Can experiments on animals ever be justified?

5.2 Non-fiction

Stories of UFOs (Unidentified Flying Objects) have always captured people's imaginations, and many popular films such as 'Close Encounters of the Third Kind' and 'E.T.' explore what might happen if beings from outer space land on Earth. Although these stories are fiction, there are plenty of accounts published in newspapers and magazines where people claim to have seen extra-terrestrial activity. One of the most famous reports is that of the Roswell Incident.

The Roswell Incident

In the Roswell Incident report, it was claimed that the American Government tried to cover up evidence of a UFO landing in New Mexico.

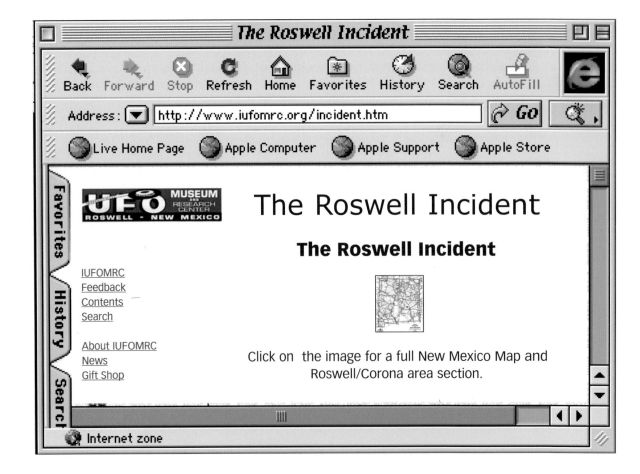

The Roswell Incident

Address: http://www.iufomrc.org/incident.htm

Live Home Page　Apple Computer　Apple Support　Apple Store

Favorites
History
Search
Page Holder

Library/Research
Exhibits
The Roswell
Incident
Kids' Club

Clifford Stone
Andy Kissner
1947 Maps
Witnesses
Weather Balloon?

1 In the summer of 1947, there were a number of UFO sightings in the United States.

2 Sometime during the first week of July 1947, something crashed near Roswell.

3 W.W. "Mac" Brazel, a New Mexico rancher, saddled up his horse and rode out with the son of neighbors Floyd and Loretta Proctor to check on the sheep after a fierce thunderstorm the night before. As they rode along, Brazel began to notice unusual pieces of what seemed to be metal debris, scattered over a large area. Upon further inspection, Brazel saw that a shallow trench, several hundred feet long, had been gouged into the land.

4 Brazel was struck by the unusual properties of the debris, and after dragging a large piece of it to a shed, he took some of it over to show the Proctors. Mrs. Proctor has recently (as of June 1997) moved from the ranch into a home nearer to town, but she remembers Mac showing up with strange material.

5 The Proctors told Brazel that he might be holding wreckage from a UFO or a government project, and that he should report the incident to the sheriff. A day or two later, Mac drove into Roswell where he reported the incident to Sheriff George Wilcox, who reported it to Intelligence Officer, Major Jesse Marcel of the 509 Bomb Group, and for days thereafter, the debris site was closed while the wreckage was cleared.

6 On July 8, 1947, a press release stating that the wreckage of a crashed disk had been recovered was issued by the Commander of the 509th Bomb Group at Roswell, Col. William Blanchard.

7 Hours later the first press release was rescinded and the second press release stated that the 509th Bomb Group had mistakenly identified a weather balloon as wreckage of a flying saucer.

Internet zone

Address: http://www.iufomrc.org/incident.htm

Live Home Page — Apple Computer — Apple Support — Apple Store

8 Meanwhile, back in Roswell, Glenn Dennis, a young mortician working at the Ballard Funeral Home, received some curious calls one afternoon from the morgue at the air field. It seems the Mortuary Officer needed to get a hold of some small hermetically sealed coffins, and wanted information about how to preserve bodies that had been exposed to the elements for a few days, without contaminating the tissue.

9 Glenn Dennis drove out to the base hospital later that evening where he saw large pieces of wreckage with strange engravings on one of the pieces sticking out of the back of a military ambulance. Upon entering the hospital he started to visit with a nurse he knew, when suddenly he was threatened by military police and forced to leave.

10 The next day, Glenn Dennis met with the nurse. She told him about the bodies and drew pictures of them on a prescription pad. Within a few days she was transferred to England, her whereabouts still unknown.

11 According to the research of Don Schmitt and Kevin Randle, in their book, A History of UFO Crashes, from which the following account of the Roswell Incident, in part, is based, the military had been watching an unidentified flying object on radar for four days in southern New Mexico. On the night of July 4, 1947, radar indicated that the object was down around thirty to forty miles northwest of Roswell.

12 Eye witness William Woody, who lived east of Roswell, remembered being outside with his father the night of July 4, 1947, when he saw a brilliant object plunge to the ground. A couple of days later when Woody and his father tried to locate the area of the crash, they were stopped by military personnel, who had cordoned off the area.

13 Acting on the call from Sheriff Wilcox, Intelligence Officer, Major Jesse Marcel was sent by Col. William Blanchard, to investigate Mac Brazel's story.

14 Marcel and Senior Counter Intelligence Corps (CIC) agent, Captain Sheridan Cavitt, followed a rancher off-road to his place. They spent the night there and Marcel inspected a large piece of debris that Brazel had dragged from the pasture.

Internet zone

Address: http://www.iufomrc.org/incident.htm Go

Live Home Page   Apple Computer   Apple Support   Apple Store

Favorites | History | Search | Page Holder

15 Monday morning, July 7, 1947, Major Jesse Marcel took his first step onto the debris field. Marcel would remark later that "something... must have exploded above the ground and fell." As Brazel, Cavitt and Marcel inspected the field, Marcel was able to "determine which direction it came from, and which direction it was heading. It was in the pattern... you could tell where it started out and where it ended by how it was thinned out..."

16 According to Marcel, the debris was "strewn over a wide area, I guess maybe three-quarters of a mile long and a few hundred feet wide." Scattered in the debris were small bits of metal that Marcel held a cigarette lighter to, to see if it would burn. "I lit the cigarette lighter to some of this stuff and it didn't burn," he said.

17 Along with the metal, Marcel described weightless I-beam-like structures that were 3/8" x 1/4", none of them very long, that would neither bend nor break. Some of these I-beams had indecipherable characters along the length, in two colors. Marcel also described metal debris the thickness of tin foil that was indestructible.

18 After gathering enough debris to fill his staff car, Maj. Marcel decided to stop by his home on the way back to the base so that he could show his family the unusual debris. He'd never seen anything quite like it. "I didn't know what we were picking up. I still don't know what it was...it could not have been part of an aircraft, not part of any kind of weather balloon or experimental balloon...I've seen rockets...sent up at the White Sands Testing Grounds. It definitely was not part of an aircraft or missile or rocket."

19 Under hypnosis conducted by Dr. John Watkins in May of 1990, Jesse Marcel Jr. remembered being awakened by his father that night and following him outside to help carry in a large box filled with debris. Once inside, they emptied the contents of the debris onto the kitchen floor.

20 Jesse Jr. described the lead foil and I-beams. Under hypnosis, he recalled the writing on the I-beams as "Purple. Strange. Never saw anything like it...Different geometric shapes, leaves and circles." Under questioning, Jesse Jr. said the symbols were shiny purple and they were small. There were many separate figures. This too, under hypnosis: [Marcel Sr. was saying it was a flying saucer] "I ask him what a flying saucer is. I don't know what a flying saucer is...It's a ship. [Dad's] excited!"

Internet zone

223

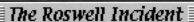 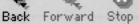      

Back Forward Stop Refresh Home Favorites History Search AutoFill

Address: http://www.iufomrc.org/incident.htm   Go

Live Home Page   Apple Computer   Apple Support   Apple Store

Roswell Daily Record

RAAF Captures Flying Saucer On Ranch in Roswell Region

21 At 11:00 A.M. Walter Haut, public relations officer, finished the press release he'd been ordered to write, and gave copies of the release to the two radio stations and both of the newspapers. By 2:26 P.M., the story was out on the AP wire:

22 "The Army Air Forces here today announced a flying disk had been found."

23 As calls began to pour into the base from all over the world, Lt. Robert Shirkey watched as MPs carried loaded wreckage onto a C-54 from the First Transport Unit.

24 To get a better look, Shirkey stepped around Col. Blanchard, who was irritated with all of the calls coming into the base. Blanchard decided to travel out to the debris field and left instructions that he'd gone on leave.

25 On the morning of July 8, Marcel reported what he'd found to Col. Blanchard, showing him pieces of the wreckage, none of which looked like anything Blanchard had ever seen. Blanchard then sent Marcel to Carswell [Fort Worth Army Air Field] to see General Ramey, Commanding Officer of the Eighth Air Force.

26 Marcel stated years later to Walter Haut that he'd taken some of the debris into Ramey's office to show him what had been found. The material was displayed on Ramey's desk for the general when he returned.

27 Upon his return, General Ramey wanted to see the exact location of the debris field, so he and Marcel went to the map room down the hall–but when they returned, the wreckage that had been placed on the desk was gone and a weather balloon was spread out on the floor. Major Charles A. Cashon took the now-famous photo of Marcel with the weather balloon, in General Ramey's office.

Internet zone

The Roswell Incident

http://www.iufomrc.org/incident.htm

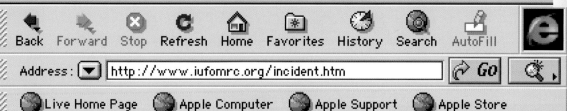

Live Home Page   Apple Computer   Apple Support   Apple Store

Jesse Marcel with the weather balloon.
As published in *UFO Crash at Roswell*
by Kevin D. Randle and Donald R. Schmitt.
(Photo courtesy of Fort Worth Star - Telegram Photographic Collection, Special Collections division,
University of Texas at Arlington Libraries)

28 It was then reported that General Ramey recognized the remains as part of a weather balloon. Brigadier General Thomas DuBose, the chief of staff of the Eighth Air Force, said, "[It] was a cover story. The whole balloon part of it. That was the part of the story we were told to give to the public and news and that was it."

29 The military tried to convince the news media from that day forward that the object found near Roswell was nothing more than a weather balloon.

30 July 9, as reports went out that the crashed object was actually a weather balloon, clean-up crews were busily clearing the debris. Bud Payne, a rancher at Corona, was trying to round up a stray when he was spotted by military and carried off the Foster ranch, and Jud Roberts along with Walt Whitmore were turned away as they approached the debris field.

31 As the wreckage was brought to the base, it was crated and stored in a hangar.

32 Back in town, Walt Whitmore and Lyman Strickland saw their friend, Mac Brazel, who was being escorted to the Roswell Daily Record by three military officers. He ignored Whitmore and Strickland, which was not at all like Mac, and once he got to the Roswell Daily Record offices, he changed his story. He now claimed to have found the debris on June 14. Brazel also mentioned that he'd found weather observation devices on two other occasions, but what he found this time was no weather balloon.

Internet zone

Back Forward Stop Refresh Home Favorites History Search AutoFill

Address: http://www.iufomrc.org/incident.htm Go

Live Home Page Apple Computer Apple Support Apple Store

33 Later that afternoon, an officer from the base retrieved all of the copies of Haut's press release from the radio stations and newspaper offices.

34 The Las Vegas Review Journal, along with dozens of other newspapers, carried the AP story:

35 "Reports of flying saucers whizzing through the sky fell off sharply today as the army and the navy began a concentrated campaign to stop the rumors."

36 The story also reported that AAF Headquarters in Washington had "delivered a blistering rebuke to officers at Roswell."

The Roswell Incident Timeline

Clifford Stone: Project Moondust & Project Blue Fly

NM Representative Andy Kissner's Initiative for a Roswell Witness Protection Program

1947 Maps

The Witnesses

Weather Balloon?

Contact the IUFOMRC

Open 7 days a week
Winter (October 1 through April 30): 10:00 AM to 5:00 PM
Summer (May 1 through September 30): 9:00 AM to 5:00 PM
Free Admission - Donations Accepted

[Home] [Clifford Stone] [Andy Kissner] [1947 Maps] [Witnesses]
[Weather Balloon?]

Internet zone

226

Reading for meaning

1 How does the writer imply that the 'something' which crashed near Roswell was a UFO?

2 What does Brazel find to suggest that the debris was from a UFO?

3 Why do the Proctors advise Brazel to report the wreckage to the sheriff?

4 What three things do the authorities do in the first two days which suggest they want to keep the incident a secret from the public?

5 What features of the debris lead Major Marcel to conclude that the object could not have been a rocket, missile or aircraft?

6 Why do you think the military authorities tried to convince the media that the wreckage was a weather balloon?

7 How does the writer suggest that Brazel was put under pressure to change his story?

8 Explain how the phrases show that the writer is trying to sound as if he is being neutral:

   a) 'In the summer of 1947, there were ...' (paragraph 1)

   b) 'According to ...'(paragraphs 11 and 16)

   c) 'Eye witness ... remembered ...'(paragraph 12)

   d) 'It was then reported that ...'(paragraph 28)

9 Here, the text is organised flat and sequentially on the page. How would the organisation of a web page make reading this text different?

10 Re-read paragraph 29.

   a) Which verb shows that the writer is biased against the military?

   b) Whose confession does the writer include to suggest that the Roswell Incident was about a UFO, not a weather balloon?

Spelling and vocabulary

Locate these words in the text and explain what they mean. Add them to your spelling log.

- debris (paragraph 3)

- rescinded (paragraph 7)

- mortician (paragraph 8)

- morgue (paragraph 8)

- hermetically sealed (paragraph 8)

- personnel (paragraph 12)

- strewn (paragraph 16)

- hangar (paragraph 31)

Writing to explain and describe

Look at paragraphs 3, 16, 17 and 20.

Imagine you are a private detective who is trying to find out the truth about the incident. You find Glenn Dennis, the mortician; the nurse; Major Marcel; and Marcel's son, Jesse.

Write a script in which you interview these witnesses and they describe what they have seen.

Speaking and listening

Work in groups to prepare a special report for radio, to be broadcast soon after the first press release goes out (paragraph 21). You will need:

- a presenter to introduce the programme, give the listeners a summary of the incident and interview the eyewitness and representative from the miliary authorities. The presenter will need to anticipate the kind of questions the listeners would ask and present them to the relevant guest

- an eyewitness, such as Brazel, Mrs Proctor, Major Marcel, or William Woody, who all believe the debris is from a UFO

- a representative from the military authorities, who maintains the debris is from a weather balloon.

Writing to argue and persuade

Do you believe that there is intelligent life on other planets?

Write your response to this question. You will need to consider that:

- people have landed on the Moon, and space probes have travelled to Mars, but there is no evidence yet of life on other planets

- there have been incidents on Earth which are mysterious – e.g. corn circles; the Roswell Incident; the Bermuda Triangle

- people *want* to believe in life in outer space and this feeds our popular culture, from TV programmes such as 'Star Trek' and 'The X Files', to Hollywood films such as Stanley Kubrick's '2001: A Space Odyssey', and books such as 'A Wrinkle in Time' and 'Planet of the Apes'.

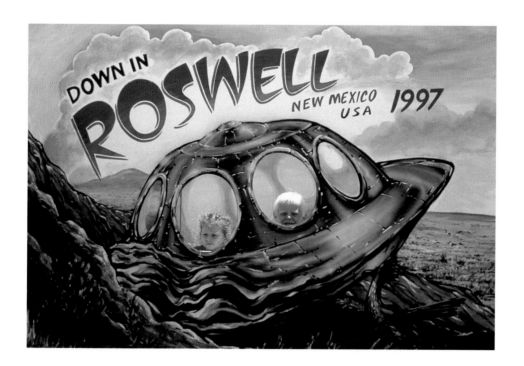

5.3 Time travel

A Wrinkle in Time

In this novel by Madeleine L'Engle, Meg Murry helps her brother, Charles Wallace, search for his missing father. Assisted by Mrs Who, Mrs Which and Mrs Whatsit, and accompanied by their friend Calvin, they travel through a mysterious wrinkle in time. As the extract begins, Meg finds herself experiencing time travel for the first time.

A Wrinkle in Time

She screamed out, 'Charles!' and whether it was to help him or for him to help her, she did not know. The word was flung back down her throat and she choked on it.

She was completely alone.

She had lost the protection of Calvin's hand. Charles was nowhere, either to save or to turn to. She was alone in a fragment of nothingness. No light, no sound, no feeling. Where was her body? She tried to move in her panic, but there was nothing to move. Just as light and sound had vanished, she was gone, too. The corporeal Meg simply was not.

Then she felt her limbs again. Her legs and arms were tingling faintly, as though they had been asleep. She blinked her eyes rapidly, but though she herself was somehow back, nothing else was. It was not as simple as darkness, or absence of light. Darkness has a tangible quality; it can be moved through and felt; in darkness you can bark your shins; the world of things still exists around you. She was lost in a horrifying void.

It was the same way with the silence. This was more than silence. A deaf person can feel vibrations. Here there was nothing to feel.

Suddenly she was aware of her heart beating rapidly within the cage of her ribs. Had it stopped before? What had made it start again? The tingling in her arms and legs grew stronger, and suddenly she felt movement. This movement, she felt, must be the turning of the earth, rotating on its axis, travelling its elliptic course about the sun. And this feeling of moving with the earth was somewhat like the feeling of being in the ocean, out in the ocean beyond the rising and falling of the breakers, lying on the moving water, pulsing gently with the swells, and feeling the gentle, inexorable tug of the moon.

I am asleep; I am dreaming, she thought. I'm having a nightmare. I want to wake up. Let me wake up.

'Well!' Charles Wallace's voice said. 'That was quite a trip! I do think you might have warned us.'

Light began to pulse and quiver. Meg blinked and shoved shakily at her glasses and there was Charles Wallace standing indignantly in front of her, his hands on his hips. 'Meg!' he shouted. 'Calvin! Where are you?'

She saw Charles, she heard him, but she could not go to him. She could not shove through the strange, trembling light to meet him.

Calvin's voice came as though it were pushing through a cloud. 'Well, just give me time, will you? I'm older than you are.'

Meg gasped. It wasn't that Calvin wasn't there and then that he was. It wasn't that part of him came first and then the rest of him followed, like a hand and then an arm, an eye and then a nose. It was a sort of shimmering, a looking at Calvin through water, through smoke, through fire, and then there he was, solid and reassuring.

'Meg!' Charles Wallace's voice came. 'Meg! Calvin, where's Meg?'

'I'm right here,' she tried to say, but her voice seemed to be caught at its source.

'Meg!' Calvin cried, and he turned round, looking about wildly.

'Mrs Which, you haven't left Meg *behind*, have you?' Charles Wallace shouted.

'If you've hurt Meg, any of you –' Calvin started, but suddenly Meg felt a violent push and a shattering as though she had been thrust through a wall of glass.

'Oh, there you are!' Charles Wallace said, and rushed over to her and hugged her.

'But where am I?' Meg asked breathlessly, relieved to hear that her voice was now coming out of her in more or less a normal way.

She looked round rather wildly. They were standing in a sunlit field, and the air about them was moving with the delicious fragrance that comes only on the rarest of spring days when the sun's touch is gentle and the apple blossoms are just beginning to unfold. She pushed her glasses up her nose to reassure herself that what she was seeing was real.

They had left the silver glint of a biting autumn evening; and now around them everything was golden with light. The grasses of the field were a tender new green, and scattered about were tiny, multicoloured flowers. Meg turned slowly to face a mountain reaching so high into the sky that its peak was lost in a crown of puffy white clouds. From the trees at the base of the mountain came a sudden singing of birds. There was an air of such peace and joy all around her that her heart's wild thumping slowed.

> *'When shall we three meet again,*
> *In thunder, lightning, or in rain?'*

came Mrs Who's voice. Suddenly the three of them were there, Mrs Whatsit with her pink stole askew; Mrs Who with her spectacles gleaming; and Mrs Which still little more than a shimmer. Delicate, multicoloured butterflies were fluttering about them, as though in greeting.

Reading for meaning

1   Describe in your own words the experience and feelings of Meg as she travels through the 'wrinkle in time'.

2   What do you think has happened in this extract?

3   What is the effect of having the line 'She was completely alone' as a separate paragraph (page 230, paragraph 2)?

4   Find the line 'She was lost in a horrifying void' (page 230, paragraph 4). What do you think has happened to Meg?

5   Find the paragraph beginning 'Suddenly she was aware of her heart beating rapidly…' and read to 'Let me wake up'. Why do you think the writer switches from **third person**, *she*, to **first person**, *I*, here?

6   How many words can you pick out which are to do with movement? For example: 'vibrations', 'beating rapidly'. Write them into the chart below and try to explain what Madeleine L'Engle means by using them.

Vocabulary	Effect
vibrations	movement that is sensed/felt
beating rapidly	Meg is nervous/frightened, her heart is beating fast

7   Meg's senses of touch, sight and hearing are affected by her experience of travelling through the 'wrinkle in time'. Look at these examples:

   a)   'Her legs and arms were tingling faintly' (feeling)

   b)   'She was lost in a horrifying void' (sight, sound)

   How many other examples can you find?

Sentences and punctuation

1 Identify the **main** and **subordinate clauses** in the following
  sentences. *Hint: Look at the use of **semi-colons**, **commas**, and
  connectives.*

   a) 'Charles was nowhere, either to save or to turn to.'

   b) 'Just as light and sound had vanished, she was gone, too.'

   c) 'Darkness has a tangible quality; it can be moved through and felt;
      in darkness you can bark your shins; the world of things still exists
      around you.'

   d) 'She saw Charles, she heard him, but she could not go to him.'

   Explain how each sentence creates a sense of mystery.

2 Look at the last sentence of the paragraph beginning 'Suddenly she
  was aware of her heart beating rapidly…'

   a) What is the effect of starting the sentence with 'And'?

   b) What is effective about the use of commas in this sentence?

Vocabulary and spelling

1 Think of synonyms for the following words as they are used in the
  passage:

   - corporeal   - fragrance

   - tangible   - biting

   - bark   - askew

   - inexorable   - shimmering

   - pulse   - swells

2 a) How many adverbs can you find ending with the **suffix** '–ly'?

   b) How many other words do you know that end with this suffix?

3 List all the words in the text that use apostrophes.

   a) Which words use the apostrophe to show *possession*?

      For example: Calvin's hand.

   b) Which words use the apostrophe to show *omission*?

      For example: I'm older.

Writing to describe

Write an account in which you describe what it is like to travel through time. You might like to describe:

- movements and sensations *Hint: Remember to include a range of adverbs here*

- what you see – colours, shapes, sizes

- your feelings and emotions.

Writing to imagine, explore and entertain

Look at the paragraph beginning 'She looked round rather wildly' and ending '… what she was seeing was real'.

1 Which words in this section make it a poetic description? Look in particular at the writer's use of nouns and adjectives.

2 Re-arrange the text into a poem. You can omit some words if necessary. For example, you could start:

In a sunlit field
They stood…

3 Write your own poem describing the landscape of a different world.

The Time Machine

This classic tale by H.G. Wells is set in the last years of the nineteenth century. It tells the story of a scientist who invents a machine for time travel. He travels far into the future and meets the Eloi, a beautiful race of people who live only for pleasure, and the Morlocks, a race of underground creatures. In this extract, the scientist describes his first experience of time travel.

Before you read

Work in small groups.

1 Discuss what you think the future is going to be like. For example, what do you think life will be like in 2500?

2 To become familiar with the language, read the passage aloud, taking it in turns to read to each other. Some of the language is challenging; do not worry if there are words you do not understand at this stage.

The Time Machine

`I am afraid I cannot convey the peculiar sensations of time travelling. They are excessively unpleasant. There is a feeling exactly like that one has upon a switchback—of a helpless headlong motion! I felt the same horrible anticipation, too, of an imminent smash. As I put on pace, night followed day like the flapping of a black wing. The dim suggestion of the laboratory seemed presently to fall away from me, and I saw the sun hopping swiftly across the sky, leaping it every minute, and every minute marking a day. I supposed the laboratory had been destroyed and I had come into the open air. I had a dim impression of scaffolding, but I was already going too fast to be conscious of any moving things. The slowest snail that ever crawled dashed by too fast for me. The twinkling succession of darkness and light was excessively painful to the eye. Then, in the intermittent darknesses, I saw the moon spinning swiftly through her quarters from new to full, and had a faint glimpse of the circling stars.

Presently, as I went on, still gaining velocity, the palpitation of night and day merged into one continuous greyness; the sky took on a wonderful deepness of blue, a splendid luminous color like that of early twilight; the jerking sun became a streak of fire, a brilliant arch, in space; the moon a fainter fluctuating band; and I could see nothing of the stars, save now and then a brighter circle flickering in the blue. `The landscape was misty and vague. I was still on the hillside upon which this house now stands, and the shoulder rose above me grey and dim. I saw trees growing and changing like puffs of vapour, now brown, now green; they grew, spread, shivered, and passed away. I saw huge buildings rise up faint and fair, and pass like dreams. The whole surface of the earth seemed changed—melting and flowing under my eyes. The little hands upon the dials that registered my speed raced round faster and faster. Presently I noted that the sun belt swayed up and down, from solstice to solstice, in a minute or less, and that consequently my pace was over a year a minute; and minute by minute the white snow flashed across the world, and vanished, and was followed by the bright, brief green of spring.

`The unpleasant sensations of the start were less poignant now. They merged at last into a kind of hysterical exhilaration. I remarked indeed a clumsy swaying of the machine, for which I was unable to account. But my mind was too confused to attend to it, so with a kind of madness growing upon me, I flung myself into futurity. At first I scarce thought of stopping, scarce thought of anything but these new sensations. But presently a fresh series of impressions grew up in my mind—a certain curiosity and therewith a certain dread—until at last they took complete possession of me. What strange developments of humanity, what wonderful advances upon our rudimentary civilization, I thought, might not appear when I came to look nearly into the dim elusive world that raced and fluctuated before my eyes! I saw great and splendid architecture rising about me, more massive than any buildings of our own time, and yet, as it seemed, built of glimmer and mist. I saw a richer green flow up the hill-side, and remain there, without any wintry intermission. Even through the veil of my confusion the earth seemed very fair. And so my mind came round to the business of stopping.

`The peculiar risk lay in the possibility of my finding some substance in the space which I, or the machine, occupied. So long as I travelled at a high velocity through time, this scarcely mattered; I was, so to speak, attenuated–was slipping like a vapour through the interstices of intervening substances! But to come to a stop involved the jamming of myself, molecule by molecule, into whatever lay in my way; meant bringing my atoms into such intimate contact with those of the obstacle that a profound chemical reaction–possibly a far-reaching explosion–would result, and blow myself and my apparatus out of all possible dimensions–into the Unknown. This possibility had occurred to me again and again while I was making the machine; but then I had cheerfully accepted it as an unavoidable risk–one of the risks a man has got to take! Now the risk was inevitable, I no longer saw it in the same cheerful light. The fact is that insensibly, the absolute strangeness of everything, the sickly jarring and swaying of the machine, above all, the feeling of prolonged falling, had absolutely upset my nerve. I told myself that I could never stop, and with a gust of petulance I resolved to stop forthwith. Like an impatient fool, I lugged over the lever, and incontinently the thing went reeling over, and I was flung headlong through the air.

Reading for meaning

1 What things does the scientist see as he travels through time?

2 Find one example of each of the following to report back to the rest of the class:

   a) the writer's use of colour

   b) references to the moon, or stars, or sun.

   c) References to the movement of the machine

3 Look at the first line. How would you describe the scientist's feelings?

4 The writer uses **similes**, **metaphors** and **personification** in this extract. Here are three examples:

simile: 'night followed day like the flapping of a black wing'

metaphor: 'the palpitation of night and day'

personification: 'I saw the moon spinning swiftly through her quarters'

    a) Find one more example of each in the text. Do you think they are effective?

5 What do you think happens next? You could consider:

- what kind of future world the scientist finds himself in

- any people or creatures he meets

- whether he manages to find his way back to his own time or not.

6 The writer says that the sensations of time travelling are 'excessively unpleasant'. What are some of the sensations he describes?

7 As a class, discuss what the writer is trying to convey in this extract.

8 How is H. G. Wells's description of time travel different to Madeleine L'Engle's in 'A Wrinkle in Time'?

Sentences and punctuation

Look at these two sentences:

- The dim suggestion of the laboratory seemed presently to fall away from me, and I saw the sun hopping swiftly across the sky, leaping it every minute, and every minute marking a day.'

- 'I saw trees growing and changing like puffs of vapour, now brown, now green; they grew, spread, shivered, and passed away.'

Wells tries to convey the immense speed at which the time machine is travelling by writing complex sentences with a variety of punctuation, and by describing how things appear and disappear in moments, using verbs and adverbs in a particular way.

I Which verbs are used to indicate the rapid passing of time?

2 What kind of punctuation does he use? Explain whether you think this is more effective than using simple sentences.

Spelling and vocabulary

1   Find these words in the extract:

- switchback

- headlong

- hillside

- therewith

These words are called **compound words** because they can be separated into two independent words. For example: 'head' and 'long'.

a)   How many other compound words can you think of?

b)   What do they mean?

2   a)   Find as many words as you can in the extract which use the prefix 'inter–', which means 'between'.

b)   What do these words mean?

c)   How many other words beginning with the prefix 'inter–' can you think of? Make a wall display using the vocabulary you find.

Writing to inform, explain and describe

Write a front-page newspaper article reporting the first successful journey through time. You will need to make up the following:

- the name of your newspaper

- an eye-catching headline. *Hint: Use alliteration.*

- the name and age of the scientist.

Include an interview with the scientist. You will need to use direct speech for this. The interview should explain what he or she saw and felt as he or she travelled through time.

Develop your paragraphs as follows:

- a short 'scoop' style revelation that time travel has happened for the first time

- a description of who, how and where to – factual details will be needed

- interview with the scientist – his thoughts and feelings about his experience; what he saw and who he met; what he intends to do next

- reflection on the implications for the future – how people's lives will be transformed.

Journalistic techniques

nouns and verbs used in headlines
use of sub-headings
bold type
capital letters (headlines and at the beginning of paragraphs)
photographs and cartoons
alliteration
rhyme
exclamations
passive voice
repetition
rhetorical questions

Writing to analyse, review and comment

1   Talk about these issues in pairs:

- how environmental changes have affected the world and its inhabitants

- medical and scientific advances

- developments in travel and transport

- how war and conflict may have changed society

- changes in education and learning

- how housing, entertainment and social behaviour have developed

To do this you will need to use language which indicates the future.

2   Write a prediction of what life will be like in the year 2500. Use the points from your discussion. Conclude by summing up the pros and cons of life in the future.

> When we are speculating or talking about the future we usually use *will*. For example, 'people *will* travel to work by helicopter'. When we want to express a level of uncertainty or probability, we use modal verbs. For example: 'By 2500, we *should* be able to live on other planets.'

Writing to imagine, explore and entertain

Plan and write a story in which you travel either *backwards* or *forwards* in time. Use the following points to help you structure your story:

- describe your time travel machine

- describe what it is like to travel through time

- explain where you arrive – think about some of the things you discussed at the beginning of the unit

- write about who you meet and what it is like where you are

- describe whether or not you return to your own time or travel to a different time.

5.4 The future

Planet of the Apes

'Planet of the Apes' is written by Pierre Boulle. The story takes place in the year 2500, on a planet where intelligent gorillas rule. Human beings are hunted, kept in zoos and used for laboratory experiments – much in the same way as humans at the moment treat animals in our world. In this extract, a journalist, Ulysse, has crashed onto the Planet of the Apes and has been captured.

The courtyard was surrounded by buildings several storeys high with identical rows of windows. The general effect was that of a hospital and this impression was confirmed by the arrival of some new figures who came forward to meet our guards. They were all dressed in white smocks and little caps: they were monkeys.

They were monkeys, every one of them, gorillas and chimpanzees. They helped our guards unload the carts. We were taken out of the cages one by one, stuffed into big sacks and carried inside the building. I put up no resistance and let myself be hauled off by two gorillas dressed in white. For several minutes I had the feeling that we were going down some long corridors and climbing some staircases. Eventually I was dumped down on the ground then, after the sack had been opened, thrown into another cage, this time a stationary one, with a floor covered with straw bedding and in which I was alone. One of the gorillas carefully locked the door from the outside.

The room in which I found myself contained a large number of cages like mine, lined up in two rows and giving on to a long passage. Most of them were already occupied, some of them by my companions of the round-up who had just been brought here, others by men and women who must have been captured some time ago. The latter could be recognised by their attitude of resignation. They looked at the newcomers with a listless air, scarcely pricking up their ears when one of them gave a plaintive moan. I also noticed that the newcomers had been placed, as I had, in individual cells, whereas the old hands were generally locked up in pairs. Putting my nose through the bars I saw a bigger cage at the end of the corridor containing a large number of children. Unlike the adults, these appeared to be extremely excited by the arrival of our batch. They gesticulated, jostled one another and pretended to shake the bars, uttering little cries like young monkeys quarrelling.

The two gorillas came back carrying another sack. My friend Nova emerged from it and again I had the consolation of seeing her put into the cage exactly opposite mine. She protested against this operation in her own manner, trying to scratch and bite. When the door was closed on her, she rushed to the bars, tried to break them down, grinding her teeth and whimpering in a heartbreaking way. After a few minutes of this behaviour she caught sight of me, stood stock still and extended her neck slightly like a surprised animal. I gave her a cautious half-smile and a little wave, which to my intense delight she clumsily tried to imitate.

I was distracted by the return of two gorillas in white jackets. The unloading had been completed for they carried no further bundle; but they pushed in front of them a trolley laden with food and buckets of water which they doled out to the captives, thus restoring order among them.

It was soon my turn. While one of the gorillas mounted guard, the other entered my cage and placed in front of me a bowl containing some mash, a little fruit and a bucket. I had decided to do all I could to establish contact with these monkeys, who seemed to be the only rational and civilized beings on the planet. The one who brought my food did not look unpleasant. Observing my tranquillity, he even gave me a friendly tap on the shoulder. I looked him straight in the eye, then, putting my hand on my chest, gave a ceremonious bow. I saw an intense surprise in his face as I raised my head again. I then smiled at him; putting all my heart into this manifestation. He was just about to leave; he stopped short dumbfounded and uttered an exclamation. I had at last succeeded in attracting attention to myself. Wishing to confirm my success by displaying all my capacities, I uttered rather stupidly the first phrase that came into my head:

'How do you do? I am a man from Earth. I've had a long journey.'

The meaning was unimportant. I only needed to speak in order to reveal my true nature to him. I had certainly achieved my aim. Never before had such stupefaction been seen on a monkey's face. He stood breathless and gaping, and so did his companion. They both started talking together in an undertone, but the result was not what I had envisaged. After peering at me suspiciously, the gorilla briskly drew back and stepped out of the cage, which he closed behind him with even greater care than before. The two apes then looked at each other for a moment and began roaring with laughter. I must have represented a truly unique phenomenon, for they could not stop making merry at my expense. Tears were streaming down their faces and one of them had to put down the bowl he was holding to take out his handkerchief.

My disappointment was such that I immediately broke into a towering rage. I too began shaking the bars, baring my teeth and cursing them in every language I knew. When I had exhausted my repertoire of invectives I went on giving incoherent yells, with the only result that they shrugged their shoulders.

Reading for meaning

1   Why do you think Ulysse offers no resistance when he is taken out of the cage?

2   Why do you think the older prisoners are allowed to share a cell, whilst the newcomers are held individually?

3   What makes Nova stop scratching and biting?

4   What kind of behaviour does Ulysse use to attempt to communicate with the gorilla?

5   How can you explain the reactions of the gorilla and his companion?

6   Why does the author choose to use the **first person**?

7   What is the effect of having only one line of direct speech?

8   What do you learn about Nova, Ulysse, and the gorillas that makes you want to read on?

9   The next line after the extract is 'All the same I had succeeded in attracting their attention'. What do you think is going to happen next?

Sentence structure and punctuation

1   Look at the last sentence of the first paragraph. Why has the writer used a colon here?

2   Why has a colon been used just before Ulysse's line of speech?

3   Identify the main clause and subordinate clauses in the sentence:

   'The room **in which I found myself** contained a large number of cages like mine, lined up in two rows and **giving on to a long passage**.'

4   Find where the writer has used these words:

   whereas the old hands…
   for they carried no further bundle
   in order to reveal my true nature….

   The words in bold are called **connectives**. They are used to link two parts of a sentence. How many other connectives can you think of?

Drama

Work in groups of three, each person taking the roles of Ulysse, Nova and the gorilla.

1 Discuss the characters of Ulysse, Nova and the gorilla. What words would you use to describe them?

2 Prepare a role-play based on this extract, from the time Ulysse finds himself locked up, to the point where he breaks into a towering rage. Your presentations should include the following aspects, which you could produce as freezeframes:

- Ulysse looking around at his prison

- Nova's behaviour and Ulysse's response

- the arrival of the gorilla with food

- Ulysse's smile, bow and speech

- the reactions of the gorilla

- Ulysse's rage.

Writing to imagine, explore and entertain

1 Pierre Boulle describes what happens to Ulysse and his surroundings in a very factual way in this extract. Using this information, produce a storyboard. Divide the extract into six sections:

a) the room of cages, with Ulysse looking through the bars of his

b) Nova in her cage opposite Ulysse's; Nova and Ulysse waving to each other

c) the gorilla giving food to Ulysse and his ceremonious bow

d) Ulysse's smile and line of speech

e) the reaction of the gorillas

f) Ulysse's towering rage.

2 Write a script in which a newspaper journalist interviews the gorilla about Ulysse. Your questions and answers could focus on:

a) how and where Ulysse was captured

b) Ulysse's appearance and behaviour

c) what Ulysse says and the reactions of the gorillas.

Writing to persuade, argue and advise

Ulysse says 'I must have represented a truly unique phenomenon, for they could not stop making merry at my expense.'

The gorillas keep him caged, and spend a great deal of time observing him and making notes to learn more about his behaviour. This is very similar to the way we have zoos and wildlife parks in our society.

Should zoos and wildlife parks continue, or has the time come to close them down and allow all wild animals to exist in their own habitat?

You should consider the following:

a) the danger some species face of extinction

b) the opportunities zoos and parks offer for research

c) differences between natural habitat and conditions in zoos and parks

d) the morality of confining animals for human entertainment.

Review

Which extracts did you enjoy in this chapter?

What aspects of this chapter did you not like? You could consider the types of activities you were asked to do, or the choice of texts you were asked to read.

What did you:

- learn and understand? Think of at least three things. They could be aspects of language, or new vocabulary, or reading a text to find out specific information.

Use this checklist to help you answer these questions and to review the progress you have made.

- **You have read**: a poem; a modern short story; two extracts from modern novels written for young adults; two extracts from classic literature; and a non-fiction account.

- **You have thought about how a reader responds to texts and how writers use:** punctuation and different sentence structures for effect; vocabulary and imagery to create vivid pictures; clear paragraphing; narrators and viewpoints; different text types such as poetry, short story and non-fiction.

- **You have written to:** imagine, explore and entertain – including poetry, diary entries, continuing a story, a storyboard; inform, explain and describe – including descriptions, newspaper articles, a report, a script; persuade, argue and advise – including a letter, discursive essays.

- **To improve your writing you have thought about:** purpose and audience; sentence structures; aspects of spelling including prefixes and suffixes; punctuation; link words to connect paragraphs; use of language such as modal verbs.

- **Your speaking and listening work has included:** a range of drama activities; discussion in pairs, groups and as a class; preparation of a radio discussion.

- **You may have used ICT to:** produce newspaper reports; draft and proofread a range of writing including poetry, narrative and non-fiction; research a range of vocabulary; use a spellcheck.

Sources and acknowledgements

Texts

We are grateful to the following for permission to reproduce copyright material:

BBC Worldwide for an extract from *Pole to Pole* by **Michael Palin** © Michael Palin 1994; **Bridge Travel Service Limited** for an extract from their brochure *Bridge City Breaks (Rome)* First Edition November 2000 to December 2001; Carcanet Press Limited for the poems "The first men on mercury" by **Edwin Morgan** published in *Collected Poems* and "Children's Games" by **William Carlos Williams** published in *Collected Poems*; the Estate of Angela Carter c/o Rogers, Coleridge & White Limited for an extract from "Mrs Number Three" published in *The Virago Book of Fairly Tales* (© **Angela Carter** 1989); David Campbell Publishers for an extract from *The Time Machine* by **H G Wells** published by J M Dents & Sons Limited © Everyman Publishers plc; David Higham Associates Limited for extracts from *The BFG* by **Roald Dahl** published by Jonathan Cape Limited/Penguin Books Limited and *King of the Cloud Forests* by **Michael Morpurgo** published by Mammoth Books/Egmont Children's Books; **Christina Dodwell** for an extract from her *An African Adventure* published by Virgin Publishing Limited; Egmont Books Limited for an extract from *Hope Leaves Jamaica* by **Kate Elizabeth Ernest** (text © 1993 Kate Elizabeth Ernest); Faber and Faber Limited for the poem "Journey of the Magi" by **T S Eliot**; Nick Hanna for his article "Just when you thought it was safe" published on the *Sunday Times* travel website 28th January 2001; the **International UFO Museum and Research Center** at Roswell, New Mexico, for an extract from their website on *The Roswell Incident*; John Murray (Publishers) Limited for the poem "Hunter Trials" by **John Betjeman** published in *Collected Poems*; **Little, Brown** for the poem "Siren Song" by Margaret Atwood; **Lucasfilm**™ Limited for an extract from *Star Wars: Episode V - The Empire Strikes Back* (© 1980 and 1997); Methuen Publishing Limited for the poems "A comparison of logs and dogs", "In the arms of my glasses", "Memory", "My doggie don't wear glasses" and "Poetry" by **John Hegley** published in *Can I Come Down Now Dad?* and "Flea poem" and "What a poem's not" by **John Hegley** published in Dog; The Pamela Paul Agency Inc. for an extract from *The Keeper of the Isis Light* by **Monica Hughes**; Pan Macmillan (London) for an extract from *Bridget Jones' Diary* by **Helen Fielding**; Penguin Books Australia Limited for an extract from *Toad Rage* by **Morris Gleitzman**; Penguin Books Limited for extracts from *A Wrinkle in Time* by **Madeleine L'Engle** published by Puffin (© Madeleine L'Engle 1962) and *Zlata's Diary: A Child's Life in Sarajevo* by **Zlata Filipovic** translated by Christina Pribichevich-Zoric (first published in France as *Le Journal de Zlata* by Fixot et editions Robert Laffont (© Fixot et editions Robert Laffont 1993)); Random House Group Limited for an extract from *Planet of the Apes* by **Pierre Boulle** published by Secker & Warburg; and Times Newspapers Limited for an extract from "Satellites put on the tail of killer sharks" by **Paul Ham** published on the *Sunday Times* world news website 5th August 2001.

In some inastances we have been unable to trace owners of copyright material and we would welcome any information that would enable us to do so.

Photographs

The authors and publishers are grateful to the following copyright holders for permission to reproduce the photographs:

The Art Archive (pages 19,20-23); B & C Alexander (pages 104, 114, 115, 119-127)
Bridgeman Art Library (pages 20, 110-111); Bruce Coleman Collection (page 64);
Camera Press (pages 119,229); Carol and Graf Publishers (pages 2, 34); Coutesy of Chameleon Design Consultancy (page 133); Donald Copper/Photostage (pages 164, 165, 167); Gareth Bowden (pages 191, 195); Getty (pages 27-31, 145, 148); Getty (pages 96-102); Getty Stone, The Travel Library (page 133); HemeraTM Technologies Photo Objects 50,000 Volume II (pages 149,230-235);
The Kobal Collection (page 152) Lucasfilm LtdTM (pages 95, 97, 102); Magnum (page 131);
Moviestore Collection (pages 155, 236-238, 240); Panos Pictures (pages 26);
Popperfoto (pages 11, 12-16, 225); Ronald Grant Archive (pages 243, 245) ; Tate Gallery/J. Waterhouse (pages 50, 93); Topham Picturepoint (pages 18, 34-39)